Ungureanu Ionu

LIVE. LOVE. DREAM

DISCOVER HOW TO TRAIN YOUR MIND
TO OVERCOME ANY LIFE OBSTACLES

Live. Love. Dream by Ungureanu Ionut Iulian

Copyright © Ungureanu Ionut Iulian 2018.

Chief Editor: Lee Caleca

Editor: Daniella Blechner

Printed in the United Kingdom

First Printing 2018. Published by Conscious Dreams Publishing

www.consciousdreamspublishing.com

ISBN 978-1-912551-09-5

CONTENTS

DEDICATIONS

For my parents Ion and Maria for teaching me the greatest lessons in life.

For my sister Catalina, she is the best in the world and because she always believed in me.

For my son Isaia, the most beautiful gift I received from God. Isaia you made me the happiest dad in the world.

TO ELINA

Use this Book to inspire you in life, to help you to shine.
You are such a BEAUTIFUL soul,
Raise your standards & you
have so much potential.
It's a pleasure to met you,
wish you success and happiness
with love &
Ionut Wach —

ACKNOWLEDGMENTS

My beautiful sister Catalina because she never gave up on me; thanks for your unconditional love.

My son Isaia Nathanel and his mum Mina, the biggest gifts that I have received from God.

My mentors around the world for their inspiration and motivation. Thank you to Max Formisano and the others.

My closest and special friends who always believed in me, for their encouragement, support, love, and help. From my heart, a big thank you to

Ciro, Ovidiu, Alina. R, Arny, Alessandra, Rachele, Mohamed, Tanya, Alex, Anthony, Davide, Carla G., and Hayden, Gina, nonna Elena, Pasquale, Alina. O, Nicoleta, Ich, Lena, Nerea, Michael, Moses, Antonello, Simone, Alin, Andrew, David, Marieke, Carla, Denise, Emma J. Perry

I want to say a big thank you and massive well done to Conscious Dreams Publishing for their support, encouragement and guidance in this fabulous journey of publishing my first book. They work with passion, professionalism and genuine interest. I highly recommend them if you ever want to publish your book.

Thank you Danni Blechner, my Book Journey Mentor, Lee Caleca, my editor and Claire Lockey, Crowdfunding Assistant and Oksana Kosovan, my typesetter I am so grateful for this experience and hope to collaborate with you in the future too.

And of course, I want to dedicate to you, my dear friend and reader, to say thank you for reading this book and passing it on to others.

Stay blessed and live, love, dream!

WHAT TOP LEADERS ARE SAYING ABOUT 'LIVE. LOVE. DREAM'

"Ionut's book is full of golden tips to live your best life. Not only does it have great concepts but it is full of very practical actionable steps from a man that took full control of his life. You must read this book."
– **Simone Vincenzi – Co-Founder GTeX –**
Turning Experts Into Authorities

"An inspirational and practical guide to transforming your life from mediocre to everything you ever wanted"
– **Michael Serwa – Coach For The Elite**

"This book is so special. It's not the classic manual full of suggestions; it's real life from a young man that went from rags to riches, from orphanage to coaching, from sleeping in the tube station to inspiring other people. I loved it!"
– **Max Formisano Speaker and Writer**

"Live. Love. Dream. is very emotionally moving, written with passion and intensity. The message behind this book highlights that no matter how dark the days are, we can always find light between the silver lining."
– **Ich Loc Co-Founder and Director of Limit Break Lifestyle**

"Inspiring and engaging – a sentimental way to help others through one's own life experiences."
– **Fariha Chowdhury – Student of Psychology**
at Queen Mary University

9

"Live. Love. Dream is a book describing a revolution, not necessarily denoting an upheaval of values but rather pointing to a turning back to one's primary origin: one's truthful and trustful higher self. Because no personal growth can fully be accomplished unless one listens to his/her senses and believes in his/her inner feelings, judgment and set of values, for they carry all treasures of knowledge one needs to move forwards. But one has to dare DREAM, LOVE and LIVE."

– Ionac Nicoleta, University of Bucharest, Romania

"This book won't leave you indifferent, Ionut's story is one of these transformational stories that will make your hair stand on end. I enjoyed reading it a lot! If you want to start appreciating your life how it is right now and to start loving yourself more, this book is for you."

– Nerea Carryon – Inspirational – Transformational Speaker – Life Changing Coach

"It's more than a book, it's a pillar created to shape your destiny. It's the perfect guide. Perfectly, it captures the 3 essentials things that we should not miss from our lives. Let's live, love and dream every day as if it is the last one. This inspirational book makes you aware that we have the power to be the best generation that humanity ever known."

– Alin Grigore – President at USR (Union Students of Romania)

"Live. Love. Dream. is a powerful book filled with deep wisdom. The combination of working on yourself physically, mentally and spiritually can really change your life if you implement Ionut's advice. If you are looking to take your life to the next level then this book will definitely help you!"

– Luke Scott – TV Show Host, International Speaker and Spiritual Mentor

THIS BOOK IS FOR YOU IF......

- you want to live a better life;

- you want to discover how to train your mind to unlock your potential and to live life in your terms;

- you want to fight for your dreams;

- you want to believe in yourself and to live your life with passion;

- you want to discover how to stay positive in any negative situation;

- you if you want to discover how to the fullest;

- you want to love yourself more and

- learn how to convert dreams into goals and results.

But…. Right now you feel confused; stuck; unsure of which direction to take; alone; powerless; full of dreams and no direction.

That's okay, we all feel like that sometimes and it is okay to honour that but you don't have to stay there. *Live. Love. Dream* will help you discover the tools and resources you already have inside to tap into your greatness so that you, too can be shining light for others.

IF SOMEONE GAVE YOU THIS BOOK

I'm sure that the person who gave you this book cares about you and wants the best for you. That's what friends and family members do, and if you bought it for yourself, that's even more powerful.

This book contains three big lessons that I learned in life and I want to share them with you in order to inspire you. So, please pass it on to others to help them as much as possible to live a better life, to love, to dream and to BELIEVE!

This guide will help you tap into all that greatness that lies within you. Are there inner resources that you might not be using? This book is designed to offer you practical tips to assist you in tapping into your potential and becoming the best person you can be so you can enjoy life and be happy.

FOREWORD

I have long been thinking about how I could best describe Ionuț Ungureanu's book: *Live. Love. Dream* and all of a sudden, I summoned the memory of a famous Shakespearean line from the back of my mind, approximately asking the question: **"What's in a name? If I name a rose by any other name, would it smell as sweet?"** and instantly realised that no matter what other title its author might have used, this book would have opened our eyes and hearts just the same way it did and was actually meant to do. This is because this book, which can no longer be considered a **book among books**, intuitively deals with and dwells on what a French philosopher of Romanian origin (Stefan Lupasco) called **"the principle of the included middle"**, according to which the process of human knowledge can not be viably accepted and supported by the dialectics of the subject – object dualism, governing the real, outside world, permanently being torn apart by contradictions of terms (as positive vs. negative; male vs. female; action vs. reaction; concrete) vs. abstract; reason vs. imagination etc.), as long as it specifically contains another third, unique element (hence the name of S. Lupasco's philosophical system) which keeps on living within humans even when they "withdraw" from the surrounding phenomenal world. This "third" specific, everlasting attribute of human lives, which we may call affectivity or love or soul or ....**by any other name**... is, in fact, a drop of the **Oneness** or **Absolute Being** from whom we, all people alike, stem from...

Therefore, seeing things from this perspective, the present book written by a sensitive SOUL who happens to be called Ionuț Ungureanu but **who** might as well be called **by any other name**, opens us to new horizons

15

within our understanding of how our living world should be, instead of what it actually is in fact. And the wider 3D approach to our external and inner reality can be enhanced by the inclusion of an extra **little thing called – LOVE**, binding the entire universe and changing everything and everyone for good and for the better…Therefore, seeing things

All we have to do is only to: **LIVE. LOVE. DREAM!**

However, mind-playing with various potential alternative names or significances which could have been used for or could be given to this book, I had to admit in the first place that, by all means, they have to be expressed in threes, (that is in three-fold groupings of terms), and secondly, that they should somehow better highlight its deeper meanings. But what or where should I start from?

Well, I think I should start from exactly what this **LIVE. LOVE. DREAM** writing is: the **life experience** of a boy and his sister who were abandoned by their parents and struggled to survive (that is to **live** in the most proper meaning of the word), making a long and painful *voyage* (that is undergoing an irreversible process of transformation) through all walks of life, until they discovered a universal truth (that is the feeling of absolute **love**), which helped them change their life course as they may have never imagined before but have dared **dream** about…

Whilst reading his life story, I wondered whether the author used the three title words of his book with different, maybe more far-reaching connotations, and I started looking for all kinds of other metaphorical meanings. The first one that crossed my mind has obviously been indicated by the author himself, not necessarily in this precise three-component order: BODY, MIND, SOUL, and it soon became clear to me, as it will do to anyone else, that Ionuţ was actually sharing to us his **life lesson**, in which he learned, as we all should do, that in order to live to one's full potential, one must take equal care of one's biological, psychological and spiritual existence. Simply because a powerful soul, permeating through all aspects of life, needs a healthy, strong-vibrating body and an open and quick-witted mind to generate and create vital force.

16

Little by little, as approaching to the final chapters of this soulful teaching about the essentials of life, I also realised that, in fact, it entirely defines a new **life philosophy**, showing how the three progressive stages of human consciousness and knowledge can actually change his condition and environment, through **AWARENESS, ENLIGHTENMENT, EMPOWERMENT.**

As the author often repeats throughout his book, it is not enough for human beings to live, but to be aware of their being and reason for being, implying that once people become aware of their truthful inner core (e.g. soul), they may enhance their transformative power by beaming its love-light into the surrounding world, thus creating new realities, best suited for their needs and serving a higher good.

And since all this philosophy is self-centered, then we could also read the present book as an **initiation guide**, gently leading us along the path to discover our higher selves through the **I, ME AND MYSELF** attitude, when we have to face some of our own minds' threats, to overcome our own fears, to get away of our own prejudices or even to live through hardships and shortages in order to free our mind and empower ourselves with a new, genuine and clear spirit expanding beyond imaginable limits.

At last but not at least, if I had to finally draw a conclusion about this book, I would briefly say it expresses the most concise equation of life's scope and purpose: **TO HAVE, TO DO, TO BE**:

TO HAVE a meaningful LIFE,

TO DO whatever it takes to LOVE,

TO BE for real, in a real DREAM !

– Dr. Ionac Nicoleta, University Professor,
Dept. of Meteorology and Hydrology – University of
Bucharest, ROMANIA

INTRODUCTION

I WROTE THIS BOOK FOR THREE REASONS

1. WE ARE NEVER TOO YOUNG OR TOO OLD TO LEARN HOW TO LIVE, LOVE AND DREAM!

For many years of my life I thought that I was too young to do and achieve so many things I wanted to but, in time, I understood that that notion was just in my mind and that the reality was completely different.

How many times have you told yourself you can't do something? Now, be honest. Who said you **can't**? The only person who told you that was YOU! And from the moment you told yourself that or believed what someone else had told you about yourself and your abilities, you created a belief system that carried the message that you were unworthy or unable to achieve the things that you desire.

Many times I repeated to myself that I was too poor to buy a house, or too young to have a happy family, or not intelligent enough to have my dream job and every time I did that, I just stopped myself from growing, learning and reaching my potential in those areas. In this book, you will learn to recognise and appreciate how beautiful life is and how important it is to experience life just the way it is!

I can understand if you did the same as I did; I don't know you (or maybe yes, I do) but I know something about you. I know that you have unlimited POTENTIAL, powerful DREAMS and a beautiful SOUL and for that reason I chose to write this book to inspire you to follow your dreams, to believe in yourself and to do everything with love and kindness.

I want to tell you from my heart that you are never too young or too old to start living the life that you have always dreamed. Living life is such a beautiful thing and a unique sensation. Ask yourself: **Do I live my life to its fullest potential?** If yes, how do you feel? If not, what can you do to live a better life, to be proud of it and to make the best of every moment? In which areas can you improve your condition?

2. THEY DON'T TEACH US IN SCHOOLS OR UNIVERSITIES "HOW LIFE WORKS" OR "WHAT IS ESSENTIAL".

Most of our schools and universities are doing a great job! At least partially. They can help students develop skills and apply for a job, but there is one important piece of the puzzle missing: **YOU!** Where are you? You may know a lot of things now and have a lot of skills. So what? There is no point in getting an education if you don't know yourself, if you don't realise your dreams and if you don't achieve your personal goals in life. Are you with me?

Ask yourself: **Where did I grow and discover myself during my school years? Or after? What did I learn about living life? Did I learn more about myself? Who am I? Why am I here? What makes me happy?** Now you know why you should read this book!

This is more than a simple book; it's a guide to discover the greatest gifts and talents inside you needed to unlock your potential, to learn how to create the life you want through the choices you make and mindset you choose to adopt.

I was one of the best students when I went to school. I did my best and guess what? Nothing special happened. My entire life changed when I started to self-educate and understand and know myself better. Reading this book will help you open your mind even more, to realise how important your life is and how many awesome things you can do!

3. MOST OF US NEED HELP DISCOVERING HOW BRILLIANT ARE.

I remember it like it was yesterday. Six years ago, I was on holiday in Italy – one of the best holidays of my life – when I met my first and favourite mentor, Max. He helped me realise that in that moment of my life I needed help. I needed inspiration and support and it was then that my life began to change! He inspired me to become a mentor/coach, someone that could help people to live a better life, inspire and motivate them to go forward in whatever it is they want to do, and to never stop growing. Before that, I was too shy to ask for help or support to discover myself. I didn't even know a person like that existed.

The reason I've shared this little episode with you is to help you understand that it is perfectly acceptable to ask for a mentor, for a teacher or coach to help you to discover your POTENTIAL, your PASSION, your VISION and MISSION in life. I had a mentor who helped me start living my life on my terms and pushed me to find the power that I own inside me. He helped me discover how much better I can become. And after years of training, coaching, pushing, hard work and failure, I finally made it! Now I'm that mentor and coach that I was dreaming of becoming. I've learned how to achieve great things in life, to discover myself, to love myself and, most importantly, to become happier and healthier as well as to enjoy life and share values with others. Now I understand that the secret of living is sharing. Now I'm sharing this knowledge with you, my friend. Feel free to recommend this transformational book to others who may need inspiration and support in their journey. My secret in life is simple: I NEVER GIVE UP! You can do the same. It may be difficult at times, but not impossible.

Ready? Let's start!

PART I

LIVE

Chapter 1.

LIVE OR DIE

THE POWER OF CHOICE AND DECISION

"You have a choice. Live or die. Every breath is a choice. Every minute is a choice. To be or not to be."
– Chuck Palahniuk

December 2004. Winter.

I felt so cold; outside there was almost 2 metres of snow. It was almost midnight and it was pitch black; I couldn't see anything. I was trying to make my way home. Although I wasn't far away from home, the journey home felt like an eternity as I trudged through the snow. I lived in a small old home without electricity. The furniture in my room consisted of a bed and a table. That was all I had at that time and I felt so rich.

Singing and talking to myself, I finally arrived home. My mum was usually waiting for me with some hot soup and my dad would be listening to the radio; my little sister was always happy when I came home. Many times were like that. Then, suddenly, I had to stop going to school and start working at ten years old to bring food home for my parents and my little sister but I didn't complain. Every time I arrived home, I was happy to see my parents and my sister waiting for me to give them something. I felt important and responsible. I was working hard with animals, in agriculture and I learned a lot from that time, so I'm grateful now for that experience.

I was almost there, close to the door to get inside and out of the cold, when I had a strange feeling; my intuition told me something, but I didn't get it at that time. What scared me was the deep and unusual silence. Usually my dad was always drunk and would try to fight with me, Mum and my sister. This night, everything was different. I was almost there, just a few more steps to get home to a bit of warmth and something to eat. I felt so cold, almost frozen, and I couldn't hear anything coming from inside the house. My heart started to pump faster and faster. I knew something was happening, but I didn't know what. I was tired after a long day working and, in that moment, all I needed was a bit of love and food.

Finally, I arrived at the door and opened it. It was semi dark in the room with just a little candle on the table. My sister was in the corner crying. My first reaction was the same as hers – to start crying. She was trying to explain to me what happened, but I couldn't understand her properly through her sobs; I couldn't understand what she was trying to say because she was in too much pain and consumed with sadness.

I tried to be strong and slowly asked her what happened. She was alone, sitting in virtual darkness and my parents were conspicuously absent. In that moment, imagined many scenarios about what could possibly have happened but what actually happened was one scenario I could never have imagined in my young mind! She looked in my eyes and with an almost whisper-like voice and no strength, she said, "Mum and Dad just left!"

I didn't have any reaction. I was shocked! My questions were "Why?", "Where?", "How is this possible?", "What do you mean 'they just left?'" But there were no answers. Progressively, I started to become nervous and agitated. I couldn't believe that something like that was possible. After a few minutes, I realised that our parents had actually abandoned us and we were all alone! That night I was born again. I felt such pain and I was suffering so much that I asked myself, **"If God exists, then where is HE now? Why would HE allow this to happen?"** I continued to ask a lot of questions with no one to hear them, and sadly, they came without answers.

That night, I had to make a choice: live or die! I had my sister to consider and made the decision to do whatever it was going to take to keep us alive, to survive, and to move us ahead. I didn't know how; I had no dreams, no hopes, no resources and, at that moment, presumably no future. The only thing that kept me from giving up was my little sister. She was a child who needed help and food, support and love and I was all she had. So I had to become a "little father" for my sister and do my best to keep us going. As it turned out, I was fortunate to have been forced to drop out of school and get a job. At least we had that.

And the worst thing was that Christmas was close; everything happened on the 17th of December, 2004. I will remember that day forever. I can tell you now that that day has become one of the most important days of my life. In the middle of a cold winter we were without food, parents, love, and warmth but we had a roof over our heads and a meagre income. We were alive and we had each other! I didn't have the courage to tell anyone anything about our circumstances, so for more than three months we were able to provide ourselves with food by looking in the bins on the street for something to bring home. It was a terrible time of my life, but in that period I gained power. I told myself that I didn't want to live like that. It was all just too much! Those few months motivated me and taught me how to survive; instead of being my defeat, they made me determined and activated my potential.

I was suffering from severe emotional and spiritual stress and pain; I had no idea how I was going to get us out that situation, but I knew I needed to do just that! I had stopped going to school because I had to work for my family. Unexpectedly, one day, the teachers came to our home and discovered that we are living without our parents! They called the Social Assistance and Child Protection, and we were taken into an orphanage.

I had a terrible shock. I went into depression soon after that happened and stayed there for a few years. I was miserable. I felt I was a victim and blamed everyone and everything for what had happened. I even crossed the line into thinking about suicide, just briefly. I had nothing, lived in an orphanage and was feeling sorry for myself. I thank God for my sister because she is the only reason I could see worth living for. It was because of her that I didn't do anything stupid. So a big THANK YOU, Catalina!

After a while, I started to change my mindset. I had my whole life ahead of me and everything to live for. The best thing that my parents did was teach us to believe in God. During that entire period, when I had lost myself, the only thing that I had was hope of a better life.

Living in the orphanage was a huge challenge for me. I learned a lot of things, and, in time, I understood that I wanted to do something with my life, something more than the classic routine of finish school, get a job, raise a family and die! I learned more while there about how to survive and I discovered more about myself and my abilities. I had taken a liking to taking drugs, smoking, drinking alcohol and I was stealing from people's houses; this was all we knew to do in the orphanage. However, it was in there that I understood what I wanted to do with my life and what I didn't want to become. I told myself I didn't want to live like my parents had, so I chose a different way to live my life. I started to attend high school and I discovered books. I had a lot of questions and I was frustrated and hungry for answers. I took a course in psychology and I found another world; I started going to libraries and buying books to help me understand why my parents abandoned us. I was thirsty for knowledge and wanted to learn as much as I could about the human nature. The books became my best friends, and from that moment I never stopped reading books. So far, I've read more than 500 books!

Finally, I got the answer that I had been seeking for many years. We are human beings and we all, each of us, make mistakes as we learn and grow. In that moment, I realised that I'm not a victim; it was my parents' decision to distance themselves from us. I understood that I didn't have any problems and I started to believe more in my own abilities. I stopped blaming myself and went ahead to discover more about life with the goal of leading others to discover their own.

I found out later that it's not what happens to us that's important, but how we look at what happens; it's what we do with what happens and our attitude regarding the event. In that moment, I opened my mind and I understood that I can change any situation, even mine – which I thought was the worst in the world – simply by changing my perspective of that situation.

I went from seeing myself as a victim who must have done something to deserve being abandoned, to seeing my parents as being human and having made a mistake, leaving me to grow in my path as determined by me. I understood that I can do anything I want with what happened to me. From that moment, I knew I had power. I felt it and I started to push myself to do my best in everything I did.

Too many people accept their victimisation and live as an abandoned child. But they don't have to do that. I didn't. I couldn't! There was something inside me that was so much stronger than my external self; it was my ambition, courage and determination. I had made the conscious decision to live strong and loud. I was not just going to be a survivor, hanging around, waiting to see what was going to happen next. I wanted to change my world or I was going to die trying!

At high school, I became friends with just a few people in the beginning. They introduced me to the Bible and I chose to read it twice. It took me almost 4 years because is not like any other book. It is a book that needs deep reflection and space to understand what you have read and interpret in your own way. I became wiser because I started to practice life from the standpoint of the Bible. This powerful and amazing book helped me to continue to believe when there seemed to be no point in doing so! I felt guided and I felt loved because this is a book about love, not about religion.

Every day I became better and better at understanding how I could convert that terrible drama from my life into an opportunity that might transform my life in ways I could never have imagined. Contemplating this day after day made me want it even more and it worked for me because I believed, with childlike innocence, that it would happen! I have to confess that at that time I was winging it. I had no support or love; no one to guide me and talk to me about my options, but somehow I knew it wasn't impossible. Of course, now I know that this is one of the natural laws of the Universe. Putting energy into something you believe in strongly, with emotion, will work to bring that something to you. Looking back, I realise that was one of the best times ever! I learned to love challenges, to push myself beyond my limits, and to do things that other people told me I could not.

This is just the beginning of an incredible story that can inspire you to act and make things happen. Keep reading. I will share with you much more about everything that helped me grow and achieve great things in a life where no one believed in me. I will tell you one of my secrets again:

I NEVER GAVE UP! And there are other secrets you will be discover in the next pages.

Now let me ask you a powerful question: Do you want to live or die? Start today taking 100% responsibility for 100% of your life. Start taking charge! Are you living your life at your fullest potential? Are you living or simply surviving? Be honest with yourself and whatever the answer is, just make a commitment to yourself to live a better life from today forward. Remember that you were born with that power! Start using it today! Start to live life and shine because we are meant to be the best we can be! Your life will change when **you** start to change and in the moment that you make that decision, your life will change forever. I know you are already curious about what we will speak about next, but I promise to speak about you and how you can grow, become better at anything, and make a big difference in your world.

Let's go for the next level!

Do your best!

Chapter 2.

BALANCING

MIND-BODY-SPIRIT

LIVE THE LIFE YOU HAVE ALWAYS DESERVED

"To live is the rarest thing in the world. Most people exist, that is all."
– Oscar Wilde

Now it's starting to become more interesting, isn't it? I will push you a lot to ask yourself questions because this was the first step that helped me to transform every aspect of my life. Remember, if you ask yourself powerful questions you will receive powerful answers. Don't just believe me, try it for yourself.

As a coach, I often ask questions. Questions are a powerful way to allow the client to reach their own level of understanding as to what the solutions to their problems are. All the answers reside within. It is for that reason, this book is filled with lots of powerful questions that, if delved into far enough, may result in even more powerful results that may change your life for the better.

So I'll ask you again: **Are you living life or are you simply existing?**
This is one of the most powerful questions in the world.

What do you see in your mind as the life you have always deserved?
Take a break now and write it down. This is how you will know if you
are living that life or not. Taking time to reflect on this question will
help you see if you are living your life or if you somehow ended up on
someone else's path. It might be painful when you get the answer, but the
power behind this will be very useful.

Write down the answer to these questions. Take your time!

**What do you feel when what do you think first when you wake up in
the morning?**

_____

_____

What are you living for?

_____

_____

Why are you here?

_____

_____

Who you really are?

_____

_____

What makes you happy?

_____

What are your dreams for your life?

What do you want to be remembered for?

Now that you have done this, why do you think you are living the life you just wrote about? If you are living the life of your dreams or on track to getting there, what steps did you take to get there? If you are living a life simply existing, how can you start to create a change? Start today to fix it! Find ways to change everything that is making you unhappy and push yourself to live **your** life, the one that you have always deserved. You may have certain obligations, such as a job you can't quit, but do your best to arrange the rest of your life according to what makes **you** fulfilled. The only person that can stop you right now is YOU!

Start from today and don't accept any excuses from yourself. Grab whatever it is you want, but remember to first recognize that you will pay a price for this freedom, for the life you want. I realised that for everything you want there is a level of investment involved. That price could be money, time, sacrificing luxuries or going out to dinner and treats in order to step into your purpose and gain ultimate happiness. You may need to give up certain people, friends or acquaintances who are holding you back, the naysayers and doubters who are telling you it's impossible to do this or that. It may be the people closest to you – family – who won't believe in your abilities. Keep them at arm's distance until you're well on your way to getting what you want and are strong

35

enough in your convictions to withstand their negative views of your vision. Prove them wrong!

It took me years to arrive at that point where I was able to say, "Yes! I want it and I'm going to pay that price!" I struggled with myself, with my limits and beliefs and I didn't have enough courage to do what I needed to do to make the necessary changes. However, in order for anything new to come into your life, you must remove the old, and that means getting rid of your old way of thinking, the thinking that has not worked for you thus far. For that reason, I wrote this book for you, to inspire you and lead you from my own experiences. The book will help you avoid losing any more time so you can make those changes, the changes you've wanted to make for a long time. Do you want to change your job or switch careers? Do it! Do you want to change your city? Do it! Do you want to lose weight? Just do it! Whatever you want to change, **START** from **YOURSELF** and everything will change with and around you. The most important thing is to **act**. Nothing will happen unless you make it happen.

In the beginning, when I first arrived in the orphanage, it felt like a prison. For a long time everything seemed to be out of my control and for the first month I cried all the time. I told myself over and over that I would run away from there! But I still had my little sister to consider, and I couldn't see how I would be able to take care of both of us. As it turned out, I learned more about **me** in that place than I probably would have living in my parents' house with them. I learned how to be more organised and I worked a lot on my self-discipline. In that way, I was able to make the most of the situation.

One of the best things about our stay at the orphanage was that they invested a lot in my sister's and my own schooling and other activities such as football, theatre and social life. They saw us hungry to learn and discover more about life. I'm grateful for their insight. So, little by little

36

I started to enjoy being there and made some new friends. I began to realise that it wasn't that bad after all and it certainly was not like our dysfunctional home used to be!

Every single day I sought to learn something new and to be a positive example to others. The orphanage supervisors noticed that and they started to invest more in me. Because of this, I started to believe more in myself too. I began to organise projects at school and develop my skills as a leader – those skills that I already had in me. Within two years, I had great results at school and in the orphanage in general and I was an example for others. They continued to invest in me more and more.

When I was 16 years old, I travelled to Denmark. I had this opportunity as the orphanage used to choose the best child and reward them for great results at school and for being a good example in every day life. It was my first trip ever and I learned a lot. I began to understand that there is more to life. I pushed myself to study more when others were playing, watching TV or just doing nothing. I was studying and reading books and guess what? The next year they choose me again to go on holiday. This time to Austria, which was incredible. I had never even dreamt of a holiday like that! I spent a great time there with Madalina, a beautiful soul and a very intelligent girl. I always wanted to have people around me that I might learn something from, and she was that kind of person. We inspired each other, spoke about books and love, dreams and life and it was one of the best holidays of my life.

Why am I sharing this part of my story with you? To inspire you and show you that with every opportunity carries an investment. In this case, I invested in myself so much that this opportunity was offered to me. I saw that studying was good for me and might afford me a better life. I asked myself how I might become better and better. I wanted to travel more, to enjoy more and to discover more, to meet new people and to grow. I started to love that kind of lifestyle. The price I paid was in time and dedication.

In the orphanage, every kid had a mentor and I loved my first one because she was amazing. Her name was Sorina and she made me feel so important. She's one of the most amazing people I've ever met, but she moved forward, away from her position at the orphanage, and I had another mentor, this time a man. I didn't like him much at first and I found myself complaining all the time. After a while, we became friends, and I began to realise that Ovidiu had always taught me valuable things about life. I will be grateful to him forever.

I believe now that my relationship with my father may have clouded my judgement of all men and I hadn't given Ovidiu a chance at first. Can you see how old thinking can impair your ability to learn and move forward in life? But I wanted to find the good and learn what I could so I changed my perspective of him. It was when I changed my perspective, I really began to learn from him. If you want things to change, you must change first!

When I saw how beautiful life could be, I wanted to read more books and travel more. There were times when I thought life was so beautiful that I forgot I was in the orphanage. One day, I had an idea to ask for help. I needed some money to buy things that I wanted. I found people who offered me a job after school working for a few hours in their garden or helping them with things around their home. Within a few months, I was able to buy more books and some new clothes. I felt like the richest kid in that orphanage (and probably was). What I realised was that they all wanted to have the same things I wanted, but no one was willing to work hard to get it. They preferred to watch TV or 'hang out'.

In real life, as adults, most people are doing the same thing. They want a lot of new things, but they expect to get them with the same old actions and habits. No! Stop! It doesn't work like that!

I have engraved in my mind and heart my favourite motto:

"If you want something that you never had, do something that you never did."
– Thomas Jefferson

So, you need to expand your thinking and step out of your comfort zone if you want to live the life that you want. Right now, it is just in your mind and even if you live the life you always desired, you must ask yourself: **How can I live tomorrow even better than I'm living today?** This life is an amazing journey. It's the best thing that could happen to us, but only if we learn how to live it. Why not do your best? Why not be happier? Healthier? Whatever your situation is in this moment in your life, I'm sure you can do better.

One of the reasons people can't move forward is because their life is unbalanced. They move in the wrong circles or keep moving in the same circles without realising that their life is passing them by. If you are talented or smart, these qualities alone may not be enough to get you where you want to be if your life is unbalanced. To be successful, you need to set up daily priorities that not only keep you on track and are in accordance with your vision, but create a balance in body, mind and spirit. That means when you set up your list of priorities, don't forget to pencil in time for church or meditation, family and friends, work and pleasure. Don't spend a lot of time on any one thing, but keep in mind that what you **do** spend time on and the people you spend it with will impact the direction and outcome of your life. Going for the next level involves not only sacrifice, but a focus on those things that will move you forward without compromising your health and your valuable relationships.

As a coach, I always start my coaching sessions with this powerful exercise to help people better understand where they are in life, what the situation or bigger picture is and what they can change or improve in different areas of their life. I want you to stop reading now and do this simple and powerful exercise that helped me to grow in my personal and professional life. I've used it for many years and still use it today. I do this exercise every three months and have got my family to do it, too. I highly recommend it to help you with your focus and energy level and to help you do your best in anything you do! I call this exercise: "From Dream to Goal Formula". Go ahead. Try it!

FROM DREAM TO GOAL FORMULA

Answer these questions below

Where are you?

_____

_____

Where are you going?

_____

_____

Why you want to get there?

_____

_____

How do you want to get there?

_____

_____

You are here on this planet for a special reason and you need to find out what that reason is. If you want to be successful and happy, if you want to be fulfilled for the rest of your life, you need balance between the three principal areas present in every human being. This is the secret to being successful, happy and fulfilled for the rest of your life. The three principal areas present in every human being are **MIND – BODY – SPIRIT**. There are three big steps to creating balance between the three:

STEP 1 – TAKE CONTROL OF YOUR MIND

The human mind is likely one of the most powerful tools in the universe, but it can be of little productive use if you do not understand how it works. When you finally do understand it, there is nothing that you cannot achieve. Each of us has a lot of potential and talent, but if you don't work hard to train your mind nothing will happen. You must be careful about what, when and how you think because the mind is like a computer. What you put in is what you get out! You can either master your mind or you can be a slave to it. It's up to you. For that reason, this quote by Henry Ford is true: **"Whether you believe you can [do it] or you can't, either way you are right."**

What does this mean? It means that what we believe with emotion, based on our past experience or intention for the future, is what we believe about our world. For example, what I believed about my father, and by extension all men, at the time my second (male) mentor took me under his wing, caused me to behave in a negative way towards him. What I **believed** controlled how I saw life and this mentor in particular. Once I changed that belief (changed the information that went into my subconscious), my perspective and therefore my life also changed.

I started to train my mind hard. One of the secrets for success in anything is the personal discipline you put into your life. Remember that you **are** your mind, and we all act according to what it tells us is real. We're generally not taught how to use it rather than having it use us! For that reason, I started to self-educate and choose **what** to think and **what** to read. I focused on changing my behaviour and my friends – the people I associated with – and I began to become more aware about everything that was going on around me. You need to be aware of media input and social networks too. They are extremely powerful influences that manipulate the subconscious mind and can impact how you act or react, what you believe and what you see as valuable in life. Remember, you want balance in your life, so you will start by taking a look at all the programs you watch and social networks you take part in.

Your mindset – what you determine to be important – is everything when it comes to getting the life that you have always deserved.

I remember when I started to read books every day and do life-affirming exercises. My attitude changed for better, and I can see now how my life is completely different than it was ten years ago. There is always something new to learn, so keep your mind updated and never stop learning. Once you stop learning, you stop growing.

From today, start to create new habits for yourself. In this way, you will retrain your mind so the stories it repeats become positive, helping you to change in the direction that will move you toward a better life. Whatever you want to do, do it from today, whether it's losing weight, stopping drinking or smoking, starting an exercise program, spending more quality time with your children, learning a new language, or anything else you have ever wanted to do, learn or become.

You need persistence, dedication and training. Your mind will tell you it is okay to stay the way you are. The mind likes its comfort zone. But the secret is to push yourself beyond your mind's apparent limits, in whatever area you want to see change. A new habit will take about 21-28 days to develop before the brain recognises it as a habit, so persist with these changes until you feel confident that the change has taken hold. When you train your mind to see the beauty of everything in life, anything is possible and you will be free forever from the control of past thinking patterns.

STEP 2 – TAKE CONTROL OF YOUR BODY

Many of the problems or challenges we face come from the fact that we are not pleased with our bodies. More than 90% of people say they don't like the way they look when they look in the mirror. What about you? Do you accept your body as it is? Do you like it? Or do you feel as though you are too skinny, too fat, too wrinkly, too tall, or your hair isn't right? This is what happens when we lose balance – we also lose perspective.

Our body is a highly efficient machine that needs to be treated well. When we are out of balance, we focus on things that are of little importance, such as the colour or texture of our hair. Maintaining the proper perspective through a balanced life will show you that there are certain things you cannot change, such as your height, but there are things you can change, such as your weight. When you lose control of your body to illness or weight gain, for example, these are signs that you are out of balance somewhere. You may begin to dislike yourself as an extension of not liking your body. Self-esteem plummets and other aspects of life will suffer.

You want to look good, so you must care about your physical self. Plan an activity that will get you moving, if not every day, at least three times a week. This is time you will dedicate to investing in your body in the same way you invest in your mind when you read a book or learn something new. Tell yourself that whatever happens during the course of your day or week, you will do your routine. Make it a priority. Eventually, it will become a habit and you will feel and see a big change. You can believe this because you know very well now that for things to change you need to change first. Start to eat well, to sleep well and to live in harmony with your body. Everything is connected in this life and for that reason you must be careful with the way you handle the little things. They are the same as managing the big ones. The little things add up.

STEP 3 – TAKE CONTROL OF YOUR SPIRIT

It's important that your mind and body work very well together. Whatever your religion, it has nothing to do with your spiritual level of awareness. You must pay more attention to your spiritual growth; meditate more and do whatever it takes to develop and promote growth in this area. Most of us are good with our body and mind, but we suffer in this critical area. You need to be focused and disciplined to become connected to your spirit. You need to believe and have faith in your beliefs and the things you've aspired to if you want to move forward. You need to connect with something stronger than you in this physical form, to reach that power that's inside of you. When you become more connected to our spirit or essence, you will understand that all the problems and challenges in your life are tools or stepping stones that will help you grow and learn the lessons you need to cultivate and change your life.

From today, start to care more about your spiritual life. Dedicate more time to and invest in your spiritual growth. It is one of the best things you can do to learn and then teach about human nature, and therefore gives you great insight into life. When I started to understand that, everything began to change in a direction where more things made sense and many things made great sense.

Before, I was flowing with the wrong tide, that of the minds of others. But this is natural for a young person. We're almost helpless to prevent it because we must be dependent on an adult for our survival. We're born with a sensibility and as we grow, we have it more or less drummed out of us because there are so many influences around us. Some children lose their natural spirituality and innocent view of the world later than others, but eventually we are unaware that we've subverted our instincts and our innate knowledge. But they are still in there.

Becoming more disciplined in your spiritual life will help you to live your life more in the present – HERE and NOW. In reality, we only really have the here and now. Yesterday has passed and tomorrow is not guaranteed so being present in the here and now is key. When we are present, we are able to become more aware of our breathing, the rhythm of our heartbeat and become more conscious of our thoughts, words and actions. How often during your busy day to you check in with your body? How often do we take breathing for granted? Are we even conscious of it? When in this state of slowing down and becoming conscious, we can connect more deeply with ourselves and become more mindful of the choices we make and actions we take.

When you are conscious and more connected to yourself, your eyes, and therefore your mind, will be opened to a new world, as though a thin veil had been lifted allowing all the beautiful knowledge and insight to come pouring in! Organising your thoughts around your spiritual nature – coming from a place of love – will help you to understand what matters in life. You will probably find yourself being more helpful, kinder, calmer, and more aware of how everything you do impacts any part of your world. From my experience, I must tell you, my friend, there is nothing like waking up in the morning and being able to see the world from a new perspective, to be almost hyper-aware and calm at the same time and to clearly see a path for yourself and your potential.

My aim is to help you pinpoint reasons as to why you may not be receiving what you want in life and activate new ideas and paths for you to follow to receiving more of what you do. You may have already identified what may have been holding you back and may have connected with some of the solutions I have offered. That's great. However, there is still work to do!

Although I showed you the three key steps to creating balance between Mind-Body-Spirit that are and achieving the life you've always desired, it takes discipline, consistency and practise. Get to know each of these steps intimately and watch how balanced your life becomes. Work on these three key steps until you regain your balance. When you begin to see that again, you're well on your way. Difficult, possibly, but not impossible!

Are you ready to move to the next level? I'll take you step-by-step and guide you to getting there. I cannot do it for you, but I promise I will do my best to show you how to do it yourself!

Remember, we are in this life to learn and apply, so let's go deeper where things will get more interesting! My friend, the best is yet to come!

Are you ready? I'm waiting for you on the next page.

Chapter 3.

FIND YOUR PASSION

LIVE LIFE ON YOUR TERMS

"Your time is limited, so don't waste it living someone else's life. Don't let the noise of others' opinions drown out your own inner voice. Have the courage to follow your heart and intuition."
– Steve Jobs

We were born free. So how do we explain why, after 20, 40 or 60 years, we don't feel free anymore? Why? And how is this possible? Now we will go deeper and I will explain you how we born free and by growing up we are not anymore.

For the first four or five years, our parents and family have a huge impact on our personal growth. We're dependent on them for our survival, our clothes, sanitary needs, food, language, mobility and almost 100% of all the input that goes to our brain including colours, light and darkness, sounds, voice tones, and smells.

By six years old, most children enter school and have their first real interaction with a society of their peers. Other adults enter our lives as authority figures. There are rules to follow and a structure in place. New ideas are presented academically, creatively and authoritatively. Around age seven or eight, we are become more self-reliant and it may seem to us as though everyone is telling us what to do and how to do things. We are beginning to think independently, but still don't have the authority we need to live life on our terms. We are still 'dependent' for a place to live and food to eat. So once again, our ideas are squashed.

From about 16 to 19 years old, we are essentially young adults. We can begin to make important decisions regarding our own life. We start to see things differently, but there are still many obstacles in society that keep us conforming to rules. If we are aware, we can start early to regain our innate knowledge and realise that life can be lived from a different point of view.

I wanted to share this with you so you understand that from the beginning, from the day you were born, your life has been controlled 100% by others and you had no voice. And now, whatever your age, you can make the decision to continue to live someone else's life or take back the life that was intended for you, living by a different set of rules, your own; rules that guide you in your journey instead of diverting you from your path.

Ask yourself if the rules and terms you live by are your own. If the answer is yes, you're already a free spirit, but if it was **no**, work more on setting priorities to determine how much time you can make available in your day to balance your life. Then spend more time doing the things that lead you in the direction **you** want to go. For example, you may not be able to quit your job and pursue your dream job right now, but you can start by writing down what pursuing your dream job and quitting your job would entail. When you see the pieces, you can focus on taking care of the obstacles one at a time.

If your answer was **no** and you can't figure out where or how to begin, you'll need to go deeper into your belief system, something that is also heavily influenced by your childhood. We'll talk more about this later, but for now, know that what you believe in and value can work proactively or negatively for you. A history of negative experiences can limit your growth, but there is a way to change even that!

But let me ask you: What does it mean for you to live on your terms? To feel free? To have a lot of money? To be happy? To have a good career? Be honest with yourself so you better understand if your life is on hold and you need to make some changes or if you're really happy, not just putting on a happy face.

You may go through life from one job or career to another, earning a living and learning, but never really feeling fulfilled. Until you discover your PASSION! My friend, the truth is that once you discover and pursue something you're passionate about, whatever it is for you, you will begin to live your life on your terms and you will be happy forever. Seriously. That's just the way the universe works. And if you have a particular talent, the best thing you can do is convert your talent into your passion. If you can then turn your passion into a lucrative job, you'll never have to work even one day more in your life.

Can you see how powerful passion is?

Now answer me this question: **Have you found your passion?** If yes, are you enjoying it? Are you practicing it? If not, what are you waiting for? Remember that you can live your life on your terms and you can be free when you find your passion.

When you find the clarity to know where you are, nothing will stop you. But before you can become unstoppable you need to know what you're starting; before you can follow your passion you need to find it!

To help you find your passion I have a few exercises that will inspire you and give more clarity:

EXERCISE 1: REVISIT YOUR CHILDHOOD. WHAT DID YOU LOVE TO DO?

It is so sad how we, as adults, have become disconnected from our childhood. Try to reconnect with the things you loved to do or what you wanted to become. Ask yourself:

What did I love to do?

_____

_____

_____

Why did I want that?

_____

_____

_____

Do I still want that now? Why or why not?

_____

_____

_____

It's helpful to make a list with all the things you loved to do. This is a powerful often eye-opening exercise. When I did it for the first time, I remembered wanting to become someone who would help people, but I didn't know exactly what form that would take; I was thinking of becoming a doctor, a policeman or a teacher, and in the end, I become a coach and mentor. Now I'm helping people. This was my passion from the beginning: **to help others**. I didn't know how or where or when I would do it, but I was thrilled to find out I had always wanted this!

How do you feel now? It takes a lot of courage to work on this and a lot more to follow it! You need to be a bit crazy and willing to feel a bit foolish if you want to be free to live your life on your terms!

EXERCISE 2: MAKE A CREATIVITY BOARD

Now that you know your passion, take a large poster board and put your passion in the middle. You can write it in big letters. Around it, put words, images, questions, or anything else that will give you inspiration. The idea behind this is to have a clear image of who you want to become or what you want to create. Your awareness and passion will grow because of the images and words you'll see every day on your creativity board. It will give you energy every day and motivate you to work harder for what you want!

In my room I have a creativity board and another one that I will talk to you about later. Don't just believe what I'm telling you; do it for yourself to discover the difference this simple inspirational project can be.

EXERCISE 3. MAKE A LIST WITH THINGS THAT YOU LOVE

Now make a list with ten things that you love to do or would love to do if you had the proper resources. Put down things you like, your talents or skills, the activities you like, and, most importantly, write down what you would be willing to do all your life even if you did it for free. Think about what you would like to do if you had all the money in this world and you didn't have to work one more day.

Look over your lists and try to find some common denominator. Look for things that overlap or might overlap in a career path. Eventually, you will find your passion.

If you look around yourself and the greater world, nothing of influence and importance was made without passion. Passion gives power to an idea so that it becomes more than just a diagram on paper. It is one of the underlying forces in every human being; it can unhook all your potential and help you to reach your goals, your dreams, to learn more skills, and to become the person that you want to be. And in the end, you will be living life on your own terms.

You need courage to do this; it's a big challenge. Don't look at your age or your present situation; look at the way you feel and how much you enjoy or don't enjoy life in this moment. This is all that matters.

The first time I did these exercises, I was a bit confused as to how they could be necessary because I had already received my degree in Meteorology at the University of Bucharest. I guess I saw myself as beyond or above this. At the time I did these exercises, I was in Italy studying for my master's in Aerospace Engineering. I liked it because of the opportunity for a career and good money, but if I'm honest with you, I was not feeling 'in love' with it. I found it boring and there always seemed to be something missing. I felt a gap in my heart and I wasn't all that happy. I seemed to be always looking for something 'around the corner'. I'm sure this has happened to you as well at least once in your life.

I was good for studying and had the possibility of a good career and good money, but where was my happiness? And now I'm asking you my friend: **Where is your happiness?**

This is what life is all about. Our main goal should be our happiness, whatever we do. Because I wasn't happy, I was always looking for something new, something else.

One day I found a workshop that helped people find their passion in life. I was so happy that day because my intuition had been telling me for a long time that I should do something else, but I didn't know what. And just like that I started to change, step by step. But here is one of the most important things you'll discover: **you may lose some friends, not the real ones, when you change, but keep going; stay on your path**; life is yours.

So what did I do? You might not believe it, but I quit school after four years in the meteorology industry! I stopped trying to gain my master's degree. I was a meteorologist, but I started over, from the beginning, following my passion!

That was one of the best times of my life. When I did that I was happy and sad at the same time. Happy because I felt that my life had meaning; I felt that I knew what I was doing and why. Sad because, in that moment of my life, I lost a lot of friends who told me I was crazy. They presumed to know that my new path was not for me. They told me there was no future in it and made a lot of other comments to try to stop me, but no one could. I was finally happy for the first time in my life! In that moment, I activated all the power that was inside me and I became more aware of myself and my potential.

Finding and living my passion completely changed my entire life. I had to pay a price for it and I passed through difficult moments. More than once I thought about quitting, but what kept me from doing that was that I knew where I was going and why. So, once you **find** your passion, you will know **why** you're going to do whatever it is you've chosen to do. You will need vision to help you see as far as you can. I will speak with you about the **why** (your mission in life) and about your vision; you need all of that if you want to live your life on your terms and be happy and fulfilled.

It took me years to arrive at the level and quality of life that I dreamed of because it wasn't easy to start from the beginning again, and at times it seemed to be impossible. I can remember very clearly that I had two jobs at the same time, a part-time job in a call centre during the day and an evening/night job in a pub. I worked hard, long hours during that time and I learned a lot, even if I felt alone. Many of the people in my life couldn't understand why I had done this, but I saw things that they couldn't see, and this was ultimately the most important thing.

I pushed myself a lot over my physical limits, finishing around 3 am in the pub, and I generally went home crying. I felt that because I had a degree, I should be earning more than 2 euros per hour. I broke all my limits. I understood the theory behind 'living life', but the reality of getting there was far different. Of course, I don't regret anything from my past and I'm so grateful for everything I understood at that time; everything was planned for me to grow and I believe that these things were tools received from God to help me find my way in life.

So, for you my friend and dear reader, I'm telling you from the bottom of my heart, if you want to fly high in life you need to become friends with the altitude. If you're afraid, at least **try** and **find ways** to enjoy the ride and it will become easier and more enjoyable simply because you're telling yourself to enjoy it. Push yourself to create a new attitude so that you can eventually get whatever you want. Only **you** can make it happen!

Life will give you everything you ask for, so it's important **what** you ask and **how** you ask it. Most people are not aware of this simple principle. Equally as important as asking is giving and knowing how to receive. We want a lot of things from life, but we are not able or willing to give what's necessary to accomplish short term goals. And many people will not give just for the sake of giving or helping others with no expectations. Whatever you want, forget about it for the moment and think about giving first.

Tony Robbins, one of the most successful motivational speakers alive today, believes that the secret of living is giving. Before having something you need to give something; you need to give your contribution to the world, whether it's time, studying, volunteering in the field in which you want to excel, helping others by using your own expertise, whatever that may be, and so on. This is the way the universe works – give and receive. Most people don't know this because no one has every taught them this important life principal. Once you grasp this idea, you will be on your way to having everything you want.

You may be wondering what there is to know about receiving. You ask for something, you get it and you have received it, right? Not exactly. When you ask the universe for something and work towards that end, you may still be thinking you don't deserve what you're about to receive. You may not fully believe that's out there for you, so when it shows up, you don't recognise it. You don't know how to receive. Accept the fact that you are as valuable as anyone else and that there's plenty of rewards to go around.

Most people on this planet live their entire life silently, going through the motions of expected behaviour, the way they were taught is 'the right way to do things'. They are born, they grow up, they study, they get married, they have kids, they retire and then they die, perhaps without ever knowing they could have been more, had more, done more, and left a legacy that will be inherited by their loved ones. Whatever legacy you leave, whether it's the passion in your DNA or the lack of it, will be passed on to your blood heirs. You can choose to pass on that 'lack' mentality or you can leave them more powerful then you were before you knew the secrets to life. Don't live your entire life without passion, without enthusiasm, and without meaning. Without this powerful ingredient called passion, life can be an unloving, often miserable existence.

Look at your entire life. It doesn't matter if you are a student, a worker, or a retiree. You still have time to make a decision to change everything from today forward! If you are already happy and living a passionate life, you're ahead in the game. If not, you must change NOW! Life is more than all those things that I described earlier; real living involves passion and freedom. You need to live with that fire that is burning inside you and driving you to make the best of every day. Passion means freedom so there can't be anything to stop you from living a life on your terms, happy and fulfilled.

What did you learn from this chapter? What changes are you going to make from today?

My friend, this is just the beginning.

I have something even more special for you on the next pages.

LIVE A LIFE TO BE PROUD OF

"Life has two rules: 1. Never give up 2. Always remember rule 1."

How many times in your life have you thought of giving up?

How many times did you actually give up on something?

How many times did you refuse to give up?

There may have been many occasions that you felt like giving up and, to be honest, I felt the same way many times in my life, but in each of my endeavours, the only thing I never did was quit! I've never given up! For me, it was too easy to give up and I always tried to become a better person, to become better at what I was doing, learn something new and find solutions for any challenge I was facing.

When my parents left, I had to take over. I had to change my role in my family. I had to become a little father and mother to my sister. I had to stop going to school and start working to provide food for us.

Leaving school was one of the most painful decisions I've ever had to make in my life.

In the orphanage, once you're 18 years old, you must leave. They offer you a job and a house to rent, but I didn't accept either of those. I told them I wanted to go to University in Bucharest. It was the best in our country, but they said that I couldn't go because they could not support me there. So, at that point, what I wanted was not possible. I felt that they tried to kill my dreams. No one at that time believed I could go so far. The only one who always believed in me and supported me in anything was my sister. But my determination and ambition were so strong that I didn't give up on my dream to go there, to study and to do my best.

I told myself that if there is no way, I will create a way. I left the orphanage and I moved to Bucharest by myself. I had never been there and such a big city held everything new for me. I knew a very kind person there, Alina, who helped me by allowing me to sleep at her house for a few days during the entrance exams session. I passed the elimination exam and I officially became a student at the University of Bucharest. This was my first real dream that came into reality. Here I met the most inspirational teacher I ever had. She is Prof. Univ. Nicoleta Ionac and she was like my angel during my study at University of Bucharest. He gave me books for free and she inspired and motivated me to believe in my dreams and to apply for Erasmus scholarship programme. I am so grateful to her for her support and guidance during my three years of this incredible experience. I had gained confidence and I started to dream more. I began to feel as though I deserved more and to grow more. I was determined to become better and better as an example for all my colleagues – teachers and other children in the orphanage, my sister and the other students at the university. All this happened because I didn't quit or give up on something I wanted very much!

That's just one episode of my beautiful journey called life. I remember during my studies I had two part-time jobs that helped me with food and books, with trips and all the things I needed to stay in school. I paid the price for my dream but it was worth it. This experience at Bucharest was one of the best of my life. I learned how to cook, how to dance, how to climb mountains, how to travel, how to approach girls my own age; this became one of my best skills even if I was one of the shyest students ever.

This is one of my favourite chapters. I believe that life is a gift and we don't have to give up on it. When you want to complain about your life and your situation, think about people who died younger than you, who never had the opportunity to go forward and find their passion. When you want to complain, blame your husband or wife, your kids, your parents, your job or anything else, think about people who cry from loneliness. Before you complain about your job and you want to give up, think about all the people around the world who don't have a job and are trying to merely survive. When you don't like your food and you complain about the taste, think of all the people who die of starvation or thirst because they have no clean water. When you want to change your house because you don't like it, think of all the homeless on the streets who would be happy to have a house like yours.

Now take a look at your life and ask yourself: Does it make any sense to give up now on my life? On my future? On my present?

There were a few times in my life when I thought of killing myself. I was so depressed that I couldn't see anything good or positive in my life. Many times I had to create new ways of getting through the day just to keep my sanity. But in the end, I didn't kill myself. Why? Because I took back control of my mind and my feelings. I tried to focus on the one most important thing in my life during those depressed times – my younger sister. I continued to live on for her sake. So you can see how living from a place of love (a form of passionate living) is the only thing that matters and gets you to a place where you can live a life full of meaning. If you've ever felt like this, you obviously had something that got you through or you wouldn't be reading this book. Remember, no matter what it was that got you through, you have the ability and inner strength to guide you through those hard times.

As a motivational speaker, I travel and inspire people to live a better life, and at all my seminars, I love to tell the audience some inspirational stories. Now, I want to share with you one of the most painful and dramatic of my stories just to help you understand some things better.

****

There was a girl named Anna who was blind. She hated everyone because she couldn't see. The only person she didn't hate was her boyfriend, Mike. This guy was always close to her and loved her so much! She told him, "If only I could see the world, I would marry you."

One day someone donated a pair of eyes to her. When the bandages came off, she could see everything, including her boyfriend.

He asked her, "Now that you can see the world, will you marry me?"

The girl looked at her boyfriend and saw that he was blind. The sight of his closed eyelids shocked her. The thought that she would never be able to see his eyes for the rest of her life led her to refuse to marry him.

****

Her boyfriend left her in tears, and days later he wrote a note to her. "Take care of your eyes, my dear, because before being yours, they were mine."

Of course, eye transplants are still a thing of the future, but how many times have we done the same in principle? How many times have we abandoned our values or someone special in our lives? Someone who was close to us, who loved us unconditionally and who was always there for us? How many times have we forgotten how life was before we had our revelation or before someone gave us a much needed handout? Something special, even life changing, for us?

Now, tell me again my friend, would you still like to give up? It's too easy! And by the way, it's the coward's way out, but it's often the first thing some people do when they face challenges. Remember, your brain likes its comfort zone, so the first thing it says to us is GIVE UP! But you don't want to give up any more, right? You want to become a better you and a better person in this world. Giving up is a characteristic of losers and those who see themselves as victims; they lack the courage of their convictions. Courage to fight for what you want and move forward is a characteristic of leaders. Even if you are not a leader in business, you are a leader of people, of family, friends, and most importantly, of yourself.

Now I'm asking you: **who you are?** Are you a loser? A victim of life? Or are you a fighter, a leader, someone who inspires the world with your day-to-day life? Whatever you are or want to be, it's your choice, my friend. Remember, you must take responsibility for your decisions 100% of the time. Right or wrong, all the decisions in your life are yours to make. Make them! By not making any decision at all, you are essentially making the decision to leave decision-making about your life to others.

There will come a time in your life when you will regret that you didn't try, you didn't fight for yourself, for your freedom, for your dreams, for your happiness, for your passion. I want to help you to understand that that moment may be NOW! You can choose **now** what you want to do with your life, where you want to go and what you want to achieve, or at the very least, you can make the decision right now to put ever-increasing amounts of energy into discovering what those might be for you.

From this moment forward, don't allow any more excuses! If you want to live a life to be proud of, you must oversee every aspect of it. But to do this, you need courage, you must train your mind and open your heart to access that power that is inside you! There is a lot of potential, creativity, love, and greatness in each of us. The only one that has the key to unlock and release these qualities is YOU! Once you 'get' that, there will be nothing that you can't do, so regardless of whatever happened to you, let it make you stronger. Use adverse experiences to grow and become more awake spiritually. The more you have suffered and overcome difficult situations, the more powerful you should become, providing you make the decision to take charge.

This is not taught in schools, universities, and society. That's why so many teens spend their time on Twitter or Facebook. They're looking for some connection, something to make validate them and make them valuable. But it seems no one cares about this important aspect of life, taking control of your life's direction.

Life is like a book of blank pages. Every day will hold a different story and every day you have the opportunity to fill a page with that story. Now what would you like to read about your life? Do you want your book to be the best? To inspire you when you read it? Live to inspire yourself first, then others may follow you. And if that doesn't happen, at least you will have lived a life that you are proud of! That's all that matters. The way you remember yourself and all the memories about you will be like a movie. So, which kind of movie do you want to see yourself in?

I don't know who you are, where you are from, how old you are, or anything else about you, but I'm happy that I can speak to you now to inspire you to care more about yourself and your life, to change your mindset so you can improve the quality of your life and live better, become a stronger person, and, from now on, never give up again.

I will share with you some powerful strategies that helped me to change my mindset so I could get to the life I have today.

KNOW WHAT YOU WANT

Everything starts from here. Know what you want to do, who you want to become or where you want to go. If you don't know all of this, you cannot move forward along the proper path. Your mind needs a clear vision of the direction you want to take. If you don't have that, you will waste your energy, time and resources moving in the wrong direction. With the power of focus and with a strong vision, you can achieve anything in this life.

If you don't know what you want, refer back to the exercises for discovering your passion. Create those lists now of all the things you used to love as a child, the skills you possess today and the things you've always dreamed of doing. You can also make a list of people who you believe were most influential in your life, whether you know them personally, casually or intimately, or through books or other media. When you look at your lists, try to determine a common denominator. This is the clue to discovering where you will find your best potential. This is likely where your passion lays, passion that's been hidden waiting for you to retrieve it.

Don't worry too much about how you're going to achieve your goals or get to your desired dream. Just concern yourself in the beginning with finding what you want to do. Refuse to be complacent or bored with life. When you know what you want, the universe will open all the doors for you, showing you people, resources, ideas, and everything else you need and were unable to 'see' before. Start today to define an accurate description of what you want to do with your life and begin focusing on doing the things necessary to achieve that. Knowing what you want is the first step to showing you that you don't ever have to give up again!

DEVELOP A POSITIVE ATTITUDE

So what exactly is 'attitude'? When we speak about **attitude** we're referring to the level and type of energy you put into what you do and your perspective of those things. Your attitude determines how you act and/or react in every situation. It is determined by your **perspective** or interpretation of life both in general and regarding specific events or people.

Most people are easily and unconsciously influenced by the events in their lives, and if events or people have influenced us negatively repeatedly, we will have a bad attitude toward life in general.

But attitude is everything! Did you know that? A good attitude is one of the tools and strategies you must apply to achieve great things in life. And I think it's one of the most important. What's your general attitude every single day? Are you thinking positively? Or do you have a negative attitude? Do you wake up excited to discover what the day will bring or do you hate to get out of bed in the morning because you really don't want to face the day? How do you see your future? How do you live your present?

Understand that only about 10% of all the things that happen matter. The other 90% is determined by our interpretation, our attitude and our position when we face that event. It's important to always be aware of your attitude. Remember, **what you think about often (what you put energy into) will expand, both in your subconscious and in your outer life**. Thoughts are often self-fulfilling. So if you think you are capable of doing something, you are right. Conversely, if you defeat yourself by thinking you can't do something, you won't put in the time and energy it might take to do that. In both situations, your attitude and perspective have determined your ability, at least in your mind. You will act according to what your mind believes and tells you in that moment.

You may need to adjust your attitude many times during the day, but that's okay. That's how you will eventually develop a good attitude all the time, and this is the secret. If you train your mind to develop a positive attitude and try to see the positive side in everything you do, you will make decisions with greater clarity because your judgement will not be clouded by negative influences from your past. There will be nothing that you cannot do once you decide to do it.

So, to live a life to be proud of, you need to understand your attitude, **why it is what it is**, how it got that way, what incidents or people from your past have shaped that perspective. Take control of it and use it to your advantage. Don't be too hard on yourself. Having a negative attitude some days is perfectly normal. It's human nature. The point is that if you can learn to recognize whether or not you generally have a negative attitude, you can change it whenever and as best you can. If you don't realise that you have a negative attitude, your health may be suffering and your level of stress will rise unnecessarily. Start from today to develop a positive attitude and watch how your life goes to the next level.

LEARN TO EMBRACE CHANGE

This can be one of the scariest things for almost all of us. We become very comfortable in the life we are familiar with and may feel that when we make a change, we will be incapable of fitting in, making it work, losing what we know, or learning what we need. But why are we fearful of change?

Fear is a natural and often necessary part of life. Without fear, we might step into danger beyond what we are physically able to handle. But it's fear of the unknown that keeps most of us from embracing change. Often, change will happen anyway whether we want it or not, and it's up to each of us to learn to find and embrace what those changes might bring to the table. Change is a part of life. We lose our jobs, sometimes we're forced to move, we grow old, our kids move out to lives of their own, and still we don't want to change because we're afraid of what those changes might bring. We fear what we do not know and most of what we fear may be only in our mind, but to make the most of your passionate path, you must make the change. It's the only way to discover all the good that will come of it. You may find yourself saying, "What took me so long?"

Growth is not an option for you anymore. Did I stop growing after I finished my studies? I'm still growing and learning new things. The truth is that most of the time change is for better, and once you allow yourself the possibility of changing, you'll have even more chances for your future to grow and develop in the way you want.

I'm going to tell you something that may or may not shock you. Most people want to be free, but they spend all their life in the worst and most dangerous prison ever: the prison of their mind, and only they have the key and the power to use that key to release themselves from this prison. They just don't realise they have it!

From today, my friend, use that key to open your mind, embrace change and give yourself your freedom. Freedom is all that matters; freedom to direct your footsteps in the course that fulfils your soul. Without it, if you stay a prisoner of your mind, you can have all the material riches in the world, but you will never be happy.

LEARN FROM YOUR MISTAKES

The best way to grow faster in life is to learn from your mistakes. No one can teach you how to live a better life better that you can. If you want to be able to not give up then you must get into the mindset that allows you to come to terms with the mistakes you've made and learn from them so you don't repeat them. Don't be afraid to make mistakes; we all do. Mistakes help you learn. Give yourself opportunity to at least try and even if you do it wrong, no worries. You will be fine. Next time try a different way to do it better.

But outside of the learning process itself, mistakes aren't always a bad thing. The glue for Post-Its was discovered by mistake. The 'discovery' of America by Amerigo Vespucci was a mistake. The discovery of penicillin, the pacemaker, the microwave oven, Silly Putty, and fireworks were all mistakes! Their inventors were trying to make something else, and in some cases, came up with life-saving inventions.

Most of us don't shine, not because we're not brilliant or don't have the potential, but because we stop ourselves from continuing to try after we make a mistake. Every mistake is a step closer to success in life. Don't be afraid to fail as many times as you need to until you learn. The biggest mistake you can make in life – and the only one that really matters – is giving up or not trying to begin with. In that moment you limit yourself and won't see any results.

Behind every success story there are ups and downs and a lot of mistakes. In fact the reason those people were successful is because they never stopped trying. They persisted until they found the right way to do something. If you want to become successful, you need ambition, patience and self-motivation, the last of which is the most important. If you are self-motivated, the rest will follow. If you know what you want and why, no one can stop you from achieving everything you want in life and you will never give up. It's not about giving up on something that you don't like; it's about not giving up on yourself and your dreams in life.

Start from today to be more careful; when you do make mistakes, look into what went wrong and why. Learn from it so you don't make the same mistake again. Make a list of the mistakes you make as you go along with each project or endeavour. That way you can refer to your list when you try again. This is a great technique that you can apply to anything, whether it's work, creative projects or inventions, relationships, parenting, sales, and so on. Eventually, you will see the results of your efforts and it will change your life completely.

It's all about the way you train your mind to do things; the way you approach life to make it a better life. Remember, you must oversee it! Do it now!

I used to make a lot of mistakes every single day, without realising it, and after a while I began to understand that something was wrong. I wasn't getting the results I was looking for and it finally dawned on me that I cannot have different results if I always do the same things in the same way. And just like that, I started to change every day. I improved something in my communication, my behaviour, my attitude and perspective, and this helped me a lot to become a better person. And each time I learned and improved on a certain area in my life, it built upon the previous learning.

I'm sure that you can do the same; you just need to find the right strategy for what you want to achieve and apply it. I still make mistakes now, but I've learnt how to not repeat them. It's not about **not** making mistakes anymore; it's about learning from them, taking what you can from them and not repeating them. It's not fulfilling to live running in circles, repeating the cycle of mistakes that are not working for you. Start to self-educate yourself, invest time learning alternate ways to go about anything that isn't working for you and don't give up. This is the best way to live a better life and be happier.

SEEK KNOWLEDGE

Most people expect to finish college or university with enough knowledge to go out into the world, get a job and be successful at it. But in fact, that is just the beginning of a long continual process of learning. If you stop yourself from seeking knowledge after school like many people do, you're going to stop yourself from growing. If you don't continue to learn anything new, you won't be able to keep up with the changing world and there will be no point in thinking about having a better life. You must work towards it. Otherwise you will continue to live in the same way every year, day in and day out, with a dream that never became a reality and in the end, when you're 90, you will call it life.

Life is a gift and you will discover the finer points just learning something new every day. You, as the person in control, are expected to explore life in any way you see fit until you gain an understanding of something, just like academics and becoming an expert in any field. But the game of life can be played without rules for the most part, except for the natural laws of the universe which are always in place, working for you according to your wishes, conscious or otherwise.

One of the best things to do is to allow yourself the freedom to experience whatever will help you to move forward. Learn how to expand your comfort zone and learn even from negative situations. Every experience will help you to discover a better or different version of yourself. That doesn't mean you will necessarily like everything you learn. You may find some things useful, some eye-opening, and others may only be useful insomuch as they have taught you what not to do. You don't have to hold on to everything, just open yourself up to new opportunities, methods, and theories.

Seeking knowledge is one of the most powerful strategies available for helping you stay focused on your goal. And learning – becoming a student of life – will afford you many opportunities to grow. Eventually, if not now, you will have a life to be proud of! And if you apply yourself, it shouldn't take too long.

Never giving up means that when you don't find a way, you create one. Be willing to open your mind. The more you know – the more you learn about anything and everything – the greater your life becomes with each new learning experience.

Each of us is at a different level of learning and experience and we are obligated in this life to share our knowledge. Resources are endless due to today's technology and communication, giving us almost endless possible discoveries to be explored.

I recommend that you read for 30 minutes every day. I make it a habit to do this and it's something I've been doing since I found my passion and mission. You will grow more quickly because the more you read, the more you learn, the more you learn the more you grow and you will be able to achieve anything you deserve. Most people like the view from the top of the mountain, but they don't like the climb! Whatever you choose to do in your life, one of the great secrets is to continue to seek all forms of knowledge and be an observer of life.

BE MORE PATIENT

How many times in life have you thought that everything that's happened to you was too much? More than one person should have to handle? Or how many times have you wanted to have everything very quickly? Being patient is one of the most difficult things to do in this life and for that reason, most of us are not going to go far. We are not patient with what we're doing or what we start, so we quit easily and start something else. We never move forward. We just continue to start something new with the hope that maybe this will be the thing that will give us what we want.

But you will never succeed at anything, whether you are talented or not, if you're not persistent and patient. Patience is a virtue. That's why few have it. And it's one of the most important ingredients for success any area of your life.

I remember when I started to dream and have goals, I wanted everything straight away, but with time I understood that everything in life comes to us when it's supposed to. When the receiver is ready. That's why it's important to be open and therefore receptive to new things, new ideas. I wanted a lot of things in a short time, and in the end I couldn't have them because I wasn't patient. I wasn't ready. I had to learn this lesson. Afterwards I started to enjoy life more and I focused more on focusing on the things that needed to be done in order for me to get what I wanted.

Today, we live in the Information Age and it's become the most difficult time in history to be patient. Technology and media compel us to hurry up with everything. Speed is seen as a valuable asset. It can be a huge challenge to being patient when everyone else is trying to hurry you along, waiting for the results of your work, vying for positions, keeping to time schedules, and so on. But being patient is good for our mental and physical health. Take some much needed breaks, long or short and do what you love. Go somewhere you can relax for a while and take a look at your current lifestyle. Gain some insight and awareness.

One of the best techniques for emptying your mind of all the things you're required to do on a daily basis is to write them down. People who write things down tend to get more done. Their minds are clearer to evaluate their priorities. You can make several lists: a daily activity list (take Jimmy to the bus at 7:30, drop off Dad's lunch at noon, water plants on Fridays), a 'to-do' list for special projects (till garden for spring, hem pants, shop for Christmas presents), and a list for things you'd like to do but can't really fit into your schedule right now (paint spare room, write a book, plan a holiday). Writing things down empties your mind and organizes and compartmentalises your life. This should help you to slow down and live more in the present. Start to train yourself to become more patient so you can start a life on your terms.

GET A MENTOR YOU TRUST

Everything starts from having a mentor. It doesn't matter what you want to do in life, you will need a mentor, someone who believes in you and is willing to guide you. You need someone to inspire and motivate you, to help you find your way, to support you and to be there for you anytime anywhere. Your parents were likely your first mentors and whether or not they were successful, they were charged with guiding you through your early life and setting an example for you to follow. Since you are now choosing your own mentor (and the perfect mentor may just show up for you), you can likely choose any mentor you want.

A mentor can be an inspiring book or movie, a friend, your mum, dad, or just someone walking through your life. Mentors are designed to get you facilitate your growth in a particular area of your life, but they will not do the work for you.

My entire life changed when I got my first mentor. He believed in me, told me that I have potential that I couldn't see in myself and I'm still so grateful for everything he did for me. He gave me his hand and lifted me up. My life completely changed and now I'm able to do the same with others in my way.

I've had maybe hundreds of mentors to the present day, but for me, my first one was the most real, the only one that felt real. His name is Max and he lived his life with passion and guided people from his heart. This is a real mentor to follow as an example. I will never forget this special human being who saved my life.

If you want to gain new knowledge, learn new patterns of thinking, I strongly advise you start with a mentor, particularly if you want to enter into a field where you have no knowledge or expertise. During the course of your life, you might have many mentors if you need them and there is no rule; all you need is to get inspiration. Do not copy them, just take what you need to know to build yourself and your own dreams. There is no point to copying them because you are not them. However, if they have a tried and tested formula (for sales, for example, or mixing paints or raising dogs), it's a good idea to follow something like that because your mentor would have already made all the mistakes and has come up with something that works systematically.

What I learned is that everyone will, at some point, need a mentor or coach to help them recognise their talents and abilities and to help them understand how valuable they are so they, too, can discover the beauty of this fabulous life.

BE A PERSON OF ACTION

Are you a person of action? Yes or no? It's crucial for every human being to be a person of action. You can have all the dreams, plans and goals in the world, but if you're not going to act, nothing will happen. Taking action requires courage, determination and ambition. Your life will change forever when you realise that you are the only one that must act and make it happen. It's always better to speak less about what you want to do and start actually doing whatever you have in your mind and heart.

How many times have you had a lot of ideas in your mind? How many times have you set goals and never achieved them? How many times has nothing happened in the end? Why? The answer is simple: you didn't commit yourself to any of those ideas! You must train your mind to understand that only by doing something – anything – toward a goal, even for small things, every single day, will you ever reach those goals.

Start by handling the small things in your life. Clean up and take care of any loose ends from ideas, projects, tasks that you've left undone. Decide which of them you still want to pursue by finding the all-important why. Why do you want to finish this project, or not? Will it eventually lead you to your goal? Make the commitment to finish this task. Next, you will be able to handle the big ones.

Remember those lists? Every time you have an idea, dream, desire or goal, write it down. Writing them down creates a powerful connection to your brain by adding a visual component. This is the first step to helping you to act on your intentions. (And by the way, writing things down is also the best way to learn new things. Speak it, write it, and see it. These three components help to etch the thing in your brain).

I remember myself ten years ago. I was that kind of person who was always out of control and I reacted badly all the time. I wasn't the person of action that I am today. I was always frustrated. In many instances, I acted because I was at the point of saying all or nothing. But I learned a lot and I overcame many difficult situations, not because I wanted to, but because I had to in order to survive. Life was pushing me over my limits, but I discovered a new version of myself, a better one.

I remember a day when there was no food, no parents, and just me and my little sister. We were hungry, but too shy to go and ask for food from our neighbours. However, we didn't have any other choice, so we acted. We were desperate. And out of that desperation, I discovered that I could do something even when it hurts or is uncomfortable and even if it takes me way out of my comfort zone or feels embarrassing in that moment.

Don't wait for life to put you in that position. Start from today and act to change your life. Even a marathon starts with the first step, so why shouldn't you start from today with a little step to raise your standards and go for the next level in your life. All the beauty in life and all the opportunities for you are just around the corner. Stand up, go and take them! What are you waiting for? Life will never come knocking on your door. You must step out into the world and seize it! You must take 100% of the responsibility for moving forward! You are in charge! Start from today to live that life that you've always dreamed of. If you can imagine it, you can live it.

BE HONEST WITH YOURSELF

Honesty is one of the most important virtues in this world. How many times have you lied to yourself about something that wasn't real? How many times have you repeated a story that wasn't true? Being honest and accepting the reality as it is can be a major step to changing your life. Whatever is happening in your life, try first to be honest and see the situation for what it really is. Recognise whether or not you can change and if you need help or not. Maybe you only need to learn more about the situation or gain more skills to deal with it effectively. Perhaps you need to forgive someone or help somebody; it doesn't matter what. It all starts when you refocus your attention, try to be honest, and accept the reality.

The mind is very powerful. It can make you believe something that is only true because the mind tells you it's so. Some things we know are true, such as fire burns (and even that can be subjective). Others are only true if you want them to be. It's a glass half full kind of thing. Some see the glass half full, some see it half empty. It's up to them what they want to see. So if you say 'this person hurt me' or 'I can't do that', your subconscious will continue to tell you it's so unless and until you tell it otherwise. If you cannot control your thoughts, you will forever be a prisoner of past events and beliefs, whether or not they are pertinent today.

Many times I wanted to be someone that I couldn't at that time. I suffered a lot because I didn't understand that I needed to be honest with myself, to accept the situation and to prepare a strategy to move forward. Many times I wasn't honest with myself and this habitude was transferring into my relationships. I didn't know how to be honest with the people who loved me, cared about me and supported me. One of the biggest obstacles to being honest is our ego.

Ego is the part of the mind that acts as a mediator between the conscious and the unconscious portions of the mind. It keeps you from doing something stupid, at least that's what it's supposed to do. But the conscious mind can override it. This happens when we ignore things like intuition, gut feelings, manners, or rational thinking. It's so powerful, in fact, that if we don't know how to manage it, it can work against us. If you allow your ego to take control, it will become difficult to see reality as it is and therefore will prevent you from making honest decisions or judgements.

You may think that because you have been told or believe that you have 'a big ego' that this translates to having a lot of self-confidence. And while confidence is always a good thing, it needs to be tempered with rationality and compassion. For example, your ego may tell you to prove your prowess by jumping off the London Bridge, but in reality, you are not a strong swimmer and the water is freezing because it's the middle of winter, both of which can easily contribute to your early demise.

Don't identify yourself with your ego. This is a big mistake. You are not your ego, you are not your results, you are not your achievements, you are not your house, your car, your money or your things; you – your essence – is unique and separate from all material things. Once you become attached to material things, you begin to believe that you do not exist outside your possessions and achievements. Because of this constricted view, the world outside of your own becomes veiled and you cannot be honest with anything. The idea is that you can **have** everything you want, but you should not **attach** to anything. This is the first rule of keeping an open mind.

Start from today to see things as they really are, not the way your ego tells you they are. Be honest until it hurts. It's the only way you will truly grow your soul, emotions and understanding of everything around you. Be courageous and be kind with yourself, learn how to listen to your inner voice, and once you do that, you will rarely make bad choices. In life, there are good and bad decisions, and we will only know which we've chosen when we see the results. Any decision you make should be the result of careful thought and honest self-assessment. In that way, whether your decisions turn out to be right or wrong for you, they will just be different decisions that will give you different results.

This chapter is designed to inspire you to take more responsibility of your thoughts, words, actions, and the way you live your life. If you start to practice these key strategies, there is no way that you cannot live that life that you were only dreaming of up till now. This is the book that will transform your life forever. Remember that you can **know** something, but nothing will change until you **do** something with what you know. Make the change. Transform and make it happen.

I'm sure you enjoyed this amazing chapter, but this is not everything. Let's discover something interesting and valuable in the next chapter as you prepare yourself for the next level. By the time you finish reading this book, you will be a different person, you will think differently and you will enjoy life more. You will be happier and grateful for everything.

Are you ready?

Let's make it happen!

Chapter 5.

LEAD BY EXAMPLE

CHANGE YOUR LIFE AND INSPIRE OTHERS

"A year from now you will wish you had started today."
– Karen Lamb

Are you the kind of person you want to be around or have around you? If you had to choose yourself as a best friend, would you? Most of the time we want others to change, to do the hard job, to sacrifice, to push, to make it happen because we prefer the easy way, but if you really want to live a better life, if you want to make this world a better place, if you want to be happier, healthier, if you want to become an achiever and a challenger, then you need to change first. You need to push yourself first, you need to sacrifice yourself, you need to go the extra mile and do the hard work. You need to be the change that you want to see in others, and you will inspire them to follow you, to become like you. Strive to get yourself to the point where instead of seeking inspiration, you are the inspiration.

Start from today to improve the quality of your life and make the change that you want to see in others. A year from now you will wish you had started today. Believe me, there will never be 'the right time' to do it; there is no perfect moment for you to change for better. YOU need to CREATE that moment. You need to use your inner power of choice to make transformation happen. You have the potential to create your own reality and to help others to do the same.

How many times have you had in your mind that desire to change and you never acted upon it or applied it in your life? Why? Fear? Lack of knowledge? Lack of what? You have everything you need inside you; just decide what you want, then look inside and use what you have to move forward. Going for that 'next level' or goal means whatever it means for you. Your next level goal will not be the same as mine. And no one can stop you. Your worst enemies are you, your mind, your attitude, your thoughts, your behavior, and your world view.

When I was 23 years old, I had the big desire to change my life. I didn't know how to go about it, I just knew that I wanted it. I told myself **if there is no way I will create a way**. My **desire** to change, to transform my life, was bigger than my fear; my pain was bigger than everything at that moment of my life, and this was the catalyst for change. I knew I wanted something new, I felt that I needed to go for the next level, but there was something stopping me. Something in my mind kept repeating that it was not the right time, not the perfect moment. I kept looking to others and expecting them to make that change that I was supposed to make. I was in that vicious circle of victim mentality. I didn't like my reality and I was always complaining about it, but I wasn't ready to make any decisions to change.

Growing and processing change, much of the time, can be painful. You're required to take a hard look at yourself, to actually take action and get out of your comfort zone. But my salvation was my mentors, my books, and every positive person that I had met who helped me to understand that I needed to refocus my attention on myself and not on others, to start to change from inside and to be that person that I was always seeking outside, in society. It wasn't easy, but they assured me it was possible, and now I'm the person who inspires by my example. I am crazy enough to think that I will make this planet a better place for us, with more harmony, love, peace, and happiness. Once you make that change in yourself, you'll become a light for others. You will be a mentor and you will show the way to many people around you. And by helping and inspiring others who will then pass it on, you inadvertently help those you don't even know personally.

The one constant thing in this world is change. We cannot avoid it, and the more we resist change the tougher our lives become. We are surrounded by change and it is the one thing that has the most dramatic impact on our lives. Change will catch up with you at some point in your life; there is no avoiding it because it will find you, challenge you, and force you to reconsider how you live your life. It can come into our lives because of a crisis, because of a choice or by chance. In either situation, at some point, we are all faced with having to make a decision – do we accept the change or not? I believe it is always better to make changes in your life when you choose to rather than being forced to.

You can't avoid unexpected events (crisis) in your life. And when they come, these events will challenge your complacency. Though you may not be able to control the event itself, you can control how you choose to respond to them. That will make the difference between seeing it as negative or positive. It may be hard to imagine the death of a loved one, for example, as being positive, but it's our power of choice that enables us to activate positivity. Death is inevitable, so allowing it to negatively impact you would set you back emotionally and spiritually; continuing to grieve for years over something you cannot change is foolish and unproductive. Acting on our power of choice provides you with more opportunity to change your life for the better. The more opportunities you create to change your life, the more fulfilled and happier your life will become.

I want to share with you ten strategies that helped me to change my life for good forever, and I'm sure that you can do the same in your life.

1. FIND MEANING IN LIFE

Spend some time trying to sort out what is important in your life and what is not. What is it that you want to achieve in your life? What are your dreams? What makes you happy? Your purpose in life gives it meaning and sets the direction of how you want to live your life. Without purpose, there is no meaning and you will spend the rest of your life wandering aimlessly, with no direction or focus. You will have literally been wasting your time and looking for something that is not meant to be yours.

I found my meaning in life by age 23 and I became one of the happiest people on the planet. Why? Because I understood why I am here, my purpose, and how I can do what I love to do, making me happy and others, too. Discovering your purpose is the most important thing in life; even more important than your studies, family, job or other things. Without purpose, you can't help or inspire anyone, least of all yourself.

2. CREATE A DREAM BOARD

When we were children we dreamed all the time. We were skilled at dreaming and visualizing what we would be when we grow up. We believed that everything was possible. As we grew into adults we lost our ability to dream. Our dreams became hidden, and once we started to feel like achieving our dreams, it was almost impossible because we had become so far out of touch with them.

I used to dream of becoming someone who would help people, but at that time I didn't know there was a profession that could give me this opportunity. Now, one of my dreams has come true. Using coaching tools, I help people to discover their potential, to uncover their purpose and to follow and promote their dreams.

Almost two years ago, some of my mentors helped me to create my first dream board, I was so excited about it that the first few nights I couldn't even sleep properly. I must tell you that I started to realise my dreams in less than one year. How was that possible? Simple!

First, what is a dream board? A dream board is a collection of images placed on a board highlighting all the things you wish to attract into your life. It consists of words and images that represents your hopes and dreams, desires and ambitions.

The human mind is greatly influenced by images, whether real or imaginary. Our brain works with sorting and organising thousands of words and images every day. It remembers what it sees and hears, particularly if those images are reinforced. So it may not be enough to 'wish for a villa in Italy'. You need to present your mind with an image of that villa, specifically and exactly as you want to see it.

So how do you go about creating a dream board? Clip images and words of the things you want. Be descriptive down to the color of the walls of a room, the food in the fridge, the landscaping, the boat, the dog, the money, the university, the degree, or whatever else it is you want. Look at it several times a day so your brain has a clear picture of what is expected of it. Remember, the subconscious and unconscious minds take everything literally. If it sees a picture of a boat and the words 'my boat', it begins to see this as a reality. Eventually, your thoughts (as determined by the mind) will be influenced and translated into your actions. This is one of the most powerful exercises you can do and I highly recommend it. Do it and you will see how much energy and power it gives you. Start with something small to prove the rule and watch how it will change your life and move you forward, even if it's only a step every single day.

A dream board is a great way to start believing in your own dreams again. At the start, you will rediscover what it is that you want! And seeing your dreams every day on a dream board brings them to life. Your dreams become real in your mind, because, remember, the mind takes everything literally and it will start to believe in the possibility of achieving those dreams; it will believe this is a reality because it sees the dream every day.

3. SET YOUR GOALS TO ACHIEVE YOUR DREAMS

Once you know what is important in your life and what your dream life looks like for you, you need to act and set your long-term, medium, and short-term goals. It is acting on these goals that will enable you to realise your dreams. If you learn how to set and realise goals you will achieve great things in life.

I became an achiever by learning how to set goals, and how to train my mind to get in that state of making it happen. Now I'm able to teach others to do the same. Bear in mind that your goals may change over time. Always be flexible with setting goals as priorities change. Your goals need to reflect those changes. These are the small steps you take that create the momentum for change to happen.

4. LET GO OF YOUR REGRETS

Regrets will only hold you back in life. They are events of the past that you need to let go of. The only thing regrets are good for is that they help us see where we might have gone wrong. You can rectify that now, in the present. If there is something you've always wanted to do but regret never doing it, determine if it makes sense or is even feasible to attempt that now, today. Sometimes it's not too late, but in other cases, you may have missed that opportunity and it's gone forever. At least as far as you can see right now. Don't spend time pining over missed opportunities. If you spend time thinking about the past, you will miss the opportunities in the present and the future. You cannot change what you did or did not do in the past, so let it go. The only thing you have control over now is how you choose to live your present. And what you do today will determine your future life in the same way that what you did in the past has determined what you are today.

I had lots of regrets that were holding me back. Then I came across something called the Balloon Exercise. What is it? It's simple — blow up as many balloons as you need. On each balloon write a regret and then let the balloon go. As the balloon drifts off into the sky, say goodbye to that regret forever. This is a simple and powerful exercise that works. It is seemingly only symbolic, but your mind will see it as an actual release of those parts of your past that you regret in some way. And by the way, this frees up space in your brain for better, more positive actions that will replace the old negative experiences. You can do this for hurts, regrets, misunderstandings, actions of the past, or anything else that makes you unhappy. Once I learned how to free myself from my regrets, I felt free to fly. Are you feeling in peace about your regrets and past? Or do you need to focus on letting them go?

5. CHOOSE SOME SCARY THINGS TO DO AND THEN DO THEM

This is all about you choosing to step out of your comfort zone. Public speaking is one of the most frightening things anyone can do. I was petrified of public speaking. However, I knew that I wanted to be a motivational speaker, so I joined Toastmasters to overcome my fear of public speaking. My first speech was terrible, my knees were weak, I broke out in a sweat and I couldn't stop shaking. But I did it and the feeling of completing this speech was great, even though the speech itself was terrible. I chose to keep going and now I earn a living as a motivational speaker. I am still nervous when I get up to speak, however, it is an exciting nervous and I love it.

Make a list of scary things that you would like to do, but you are too afraid to. Think about the worst thing that can happen if you do each of these things. You probably won't actually die of embarrassment.

Put a plan in place and then go do them. Never stop doing things that intimidate you. This is what makes life challenging and keeps us growing beyond our unjustified fears. And these are the things which, if we don't do them, may become tomorrow's regrets.

Another scary thing that I did was to walk on the fire with Tony Robbins, one of my mentors. Of course I was scared. I think most people would be because our brain has experienced that fire burns, right? But watching others do it, seeing that they arrived unscathed, forced my mind to reason that it's possible to do this without being burned. For that reason I did it and so far it's been one of the best things that I have ever done!

I learned a lot and I understood how powerful my mind is. This was a startling revelation!

I had become a fire walker! I was so proud of myself knowing the courage it took for me to do that. It has also encouraged me to look for adventures and new things in my life. Whatever fills you with trepidation, whatever your fears are, you may be delighted to discover that what scared you was based on unfounded fear. It was only in your mind, and now you know that you can literally change your mind by changing your thoughts, your perspective and your beliefs. Stand up and live the things you only dreamed of doing, but didn't out of fear. Start today and you will discover a more beautiful life.

6. START LIVING A WELL-BALANCED LIFE

Our health does not remain the same. Our physical, emotional, and spiritual state changes as we get older. What we can control, however, is how we feed our minds and our bodies. Living a balanced and healthy life, builds resilience to physical challenges. Exercise is the best way to attain a positive and optimistic attitude towards life because a healthy body supports healthy mental function. Living a healthy, well-balanced life with lots of exercise is a lifestyle choice that, without a doubt, will give you a happier, more satisfied and fulfilled life. It's all about finding that balance between work and hobby, between things you like and things you don't, but which are necessary. Life balance is all that matters. If you want to become happier and live life longer, focus on balancing all areas of your life.

7. FACE YOUR FEARS

It's easy to ignore our fears and hope that they will go away. Unfortunately, it does not work like that. Just because something is 'out of sight', does not mean it's out of mind. You can take this literally, too, because the mind holds onto everything it's ever experienced. But I just told you to let go of your regrets by writing them on balloons and letting them go, right? So if the mind remembers everything, how can you actually let them go? The idea is that you have resolved them now and they are no longer in control of your present.

If you want to change your life, learn to master your fears so they can't control you any longer. Our fears are only thoughts in our minds, just like our regrets. They replay like an old movie, telling us that this is real, so over time we believe that they are true. But thoughts are not real. It is our unjustified fears in life that stop us from living and enjoying to the fullest.

Fear is good when you know how to control it. But what do I mean by unjustified fears? Real fear can protect us from danger. If you're out in the forest and you see an 8 foot bear coming at you, you should be afraid. If someone has kidnapped your child or is pointing a gun at your head, you should show a healthy fear for safety. But don't become debilitated by that fear. You will take the necessary actions such as making a loud noise to scare the bear calling the police.

Unjustified fears can be debilitating also, but there is no foundation for that fear. If you've never stood up before a group and given a speech, what is the justification for being afraid to do this? Do you think you'll be laughed at? Make a mistake? We know when our fears are controlling our life because we feel discontented and anxious about doing something. Once you face your fears and realize the worst, if it happens at all, you take back your power. You have given light to the darkness of this particular fear. When you understand that the fear was never grounded in fact, then you become a free person and you can enjoy your life.

8. ACCEPT YOU

The only person who is going to create change in your life is you! And to create that change you must like yourself. There will be times in your life where you will face rejection and there will be people who will not like you, for whatever reason. Accepting who you are and loving yourself, helps you to move forward. Putting yourself down and wishing you could be better will only lead you to a life of unhappiness and discontent. Wishing only works if it's followed up by action. Find your courage, love yourself, and step out and do something crazy. Don't worry about what anyone thinks or whether it is the right thing to do. In your heart, if it feels right, act on it and go create the life you love. I couldn't accept myself before the age of 22. I wanted to, but I didn't know how. I've since learned to love myself more than anyone in the world because, after all, I know myself better than I know anyone else and have chosen to love that child in me who I see striving and trying. If this were another person, I would love them for their courage, so why not love myself in the same way? Do you see how simple, really, this is to do? Accept yourself unconditionally and start to love yourself in every way. If you have flaws that can be adjusted or changed, do it. Nothing is stopping you from recreating yourself, but be kind to yourself along the way.

9. LIVE IN THE MOMENT

Many of us tend to think that the grass is greener on the other side. Often, we get to the other side of the fence and find that this is not so. The motivation to change our lives comes from our desire to be happy. We are often so busy focusing on our pursuit of happiness that we miss the joy of living in the moment. Our desire to have happiness in our lives is a desire for a future state, not of the present. We become so consumed with all our problems and discontent in the present that we miss the precious beauty of the moment. Sitting on the beach eating an ice-cream with your best friend or partner is a moment of happiness. Appreciating and showing gratitude daily is experiencing happiness in the moment. Helping those in need brings joy and happiness to us. This is what living our life in the moment is all about – don't miss out on moments of happiness because you are too busy pursuing it! You will feel that you are alive when you are totally in the present, in the moment, just like you are right now with me, 100% right here, right now. This is the best way to live every single day of your life.

10. EXPERIENCE THE JOY OF LEARNING

Each time you learn something new, you gain more knowledge and with more knowledge, comes more confidence. Learning helps us to be more adaptable and flexible in new situations. Learning encourages us to be more creative and innovative in our thinking and we are therefore more comfortable with the unknown. Reading books is a great way to learn. To fully embrace the joy of learning, never stop reading nor searching for more knowledge. Learning adds meaning to life and this is part of what makes life worthwhile.

You have a choice to make as to how you want to change your life. I have been doing this for four years now. I read every day for 30 minutes, averaging one book per week. Reading is so important to learn new skills and knowledge. So far, I have read more than 500 books in my lifetime.

Choosing to act on these ten things will, without a doubt, change your life forever. So, what are you waiting for? Go do these ten things now! Learning is one of the best long-term habitudes you can develop. There is always something new to learn or discover. Remember that the more you know the more you grow and the more you grow the better you become.

I can already feel your thoughts about the changes that you want to make in your life. Some will be easy to do and some will require more courage and determination to change! In this chapter, we spoke about change and how you can inspire others. You don't need a diploma to become a leader in your community or in your group or circle of friends or in your city or your country. All you must do is discover more about yourself so you can be that example you want to see in the world.

After this session, you will start to act to make a difference in your life, to shine, to be brilliant, to discover you true potential and live your life the way you want, on your terms and conditions.

I am honored to speak with you on every single page of this book and I am sure that after you finish reading it, if you apply what has been written, your life will never be the same. I've prepared the next chapter for you as one of the most important of this book. We will speak about your **Mission**, about your **Purpose**, about the biggest **Why** in your life. From here, you will start to understand the real meaning in life.

Are you ready to find out why you are here on this planet? What's your mission?

Are you ready to understand your life's meaning? Are you ready to shine? Are you ready to take responsibility for your life and to make things happen?

See you in the next powerful chapter!

Chapter 6.

PURPOSE AND MISSION

HOW TO FIND YOUR BIGGEST WHY IN LIFE

"More men fail through lack of purpose than lack of talent."
– Billy Sunday

Where do you come from? Why are you here? Why were you born on this planet? Why do you have this family? Where are you in your life in this moment? Where do you want to go? Why are you reading this book?

When you start to ask yourself some of these powerful questions and begin to seek the answers, everything in your life will start changing and whatever you do will have a meaning. It's not enough to be talented, to have good leadership, to have strong skills and so on. It doesn't make any difference if you don't know why you are here; what you want to do or why you want to become the person you want to be.

At the age of 14, I started to ask myself powerful questions like these, not because I didn't know what I had to do or because I was bored, but because the pain was so great in my life that I couldn't stand it anymore. I cried every single day, I got really depressed and I had so many negative thoughts about myself, about the world, that I couldn't see the light in my life; I couldn't see any hope or future; I was broken, mentally, physically and spiritually. That turned out to be the biggest cry of my life and the one that changed my life forever.

My parents leaving was true enough and it had been a very difficult situation, but I thought I was handling it well at the time. I thought I was okay. I was thinking rationally, but in the end, I really wasn't okay! There were many times we didn't have food for many days and we went out crying, asking others for a piece of bread. This was humiliating, but I learned a lot from that. With all the problems that we had in my family like poverty, alcohol, strife and more, I never asked myself questions about life.

After my parents left, I started to ask questions about God, about life, about my family, about the world around me. My pain was too much and my heart was broken, I was completely down and it seemed everything was dark around me. I couldn't see light. These questions helped me to find my way and find my biggest WHY in this life. From the moment my parents left, it took me eight years to find my **why** and my purpose here on this beautiful planet.

The question is: Have you found your biggest WHY? Have you found your PURPOSE?

If yes, how do you feel? What are you doing? How can you improve that for the better?

If not, my friend, what are you waiting for? Let me tell you that you're just wasting your time and your life by waiting for the perfect moment to be ready. Unfortunately, I must tell you that this moment will never come if you are not able to create it. If you can't do something right here right now, at the very least make preparations. If you want magical moments in your life and you want magical things, you must lay the groundwork! Do you want your life to be magical? My friend, for that you need to believe in magic! You need to have it in your heart, to feel it, to live it, to share it, to create it!

You can have all the money in this world, you can try your best, you can become famous, but if you don't know you mission, your why, and your purpose, most of what you do will be in vain. You may accomplish a lot, but it may not be making you happy because it's not **your** real purpose. And this is all that matters in the end. How old you are and where you are from doesn't matter that much. What's important is **who you are, who you become** and **why you are here**.

I want to tell you my story about finding my biggest WHY. Ready? Are you curious about it? It was one of the biggest adventures of my life and so far the best thing I have ever done.

We are going back to 2012, Rome, Italy, when I did my master's to become a speaker, coach and trainer. At that time, I was confused. I didn't know what I wanted to do with my life. I had just one desire: to discover it and to practice it. During the courses and workshops, we worked a lot on our talents and skills, and I discovered that I was a helper. I liked to support others and inspire them, but still there was something missing. During other workshops, when we worked on vision and life mission, I discovered that I didn't have one. I was sad but at the same time so excited because I was getting set up to find it! So, to discover my biggest WHY, I wrote down seven pages about what I like, what I don't like, my skills, talents, strengths and weakness, my passions and my vision for my life. It took me two weeks to write and understand what I wanted to do with my life and almost two years to create it and put it in my heart. I did the best job ever and I recreated myself from nothing.

If I did it, you can do it, too. It's the best feeling in the world. You will feel fulfilled and happy no matter what happens in your life! It takes courage and determination, and you risk a lot trying to discover your inner power and true potential. But it's necessary in order to find true happiness and be able to share your brilliance to make this world a better place.

When you find your biggest WHY, no one can stop you from achieving what you want or becoming who you want to be. You will have more confidence and everything will be meaningful and wonderful. You will become a more positive person with a good and productive outlook.

I will show you some strategies and steps to help you find your WHY and, of course, after you read the book, you may desire to come to my seminars to get more inspiration and tools to change and grow your life further. When you've found your biggest WHY, all areas in your life will start to come into balance and you will be an example for others. You will change for better and some of the most powerful things that will happen is you will grow spiritually and become more aware of what's around you; you will gain insight into people and relationships, and you will find yourself more curious about life in general. Use your power of choice to transform your life. It's never too late.

Even in the Bible, it is said that people without vision will die. I believe this means people without vision will die inside; they will die spiritually; the light of life, the desire to live, not just exist, will become so complacent and neglected that they will no longer have any vision, dreams or imagination at all.

How many times have you given up on something before you even started? Why? I am sure you had excuses like **you are not enough, you cannot do it, it's not for you**, and so on. Why did you put yourself through all that? Because you were missing the purpose – the reason – the WHY – behind all the things that you do or want to achieve. Once you find your Mission, everything will be easier for you and you won't give up easily on things that you probably **can** do with a little effort, but are being held back from doing by fears, doubts, indecision, and the lack of vision caused by not knowing your purpose! You will become a self-motivated person and you will achieve great things in life. You will know yourself better and the reason why you're doing what you're doing. You will start to wake up every day and live your life to its fullest potential.

Life is beautiful and is like a test. But if you fail at something, you can do it again. The problem is most of us don't try again or try at all and this is the difference between losers and winners, between leaders and followers. Prepare yourself better and pass the test; there are many challenges every day just to help you become a better person, so embrace them and find the way to overcome any situation that comes up. But to do that, you need to know your life purpose and work on it every single day. Whatever you do in life, you cannot feel completely and ultimately happy and fulfilled without knowing your purpose. This should be your top priority.

There are many ways to help you find your purpose. If you haven't found your mission and purpose yet, do a self-examination. Use a scale from 1 to 10 and be honest with yourself. How do you feel physically and emotionally? Are you satisfied and happy? Are you feeling fulfilled and realised? Are you feeling like a successful person? What is it you really want to be doing, regardless of any money it might take to do so? When you've completed the self-evaluation test, you will begin to understand how valuable and how short life is; you don't have too much time to play around without reason.

Later, I will give you a list with powerful questions to help you to gain powerful answers.

Here are my favourite ingredients for developing a life of purpose. These are the steps and strategies that I learned after discovering my own mission in life, and they helped me to create myself, to create my VISION and my MISSION in this life. They will help you to find your soul purpose and change your life forever.

97

KEEP A PURPOSE JOURNAL

This is one of the most powerful things you can do! WRITING! When you write, your mind is connecting with your heart. Keeping a journal and recognizing this connection will help you identify patterns in your life which may be holding you back and desires that are latent, desires which you may have long forgotten. Writing every day like this will help you to see things that might be changed or removed from your life and others that need to come forward. When you write, you relax and empty your mind, making space for new information, knowledge, tools and strategies.

I started to keep a journal more than two years ago, and my purpose and my biggest WHY in life became evident. I cultivated it every single day. I highly recommend this simple strategy to clear out old memories that inhibit your imagination for things you desire. Our memory may be limited, but our imagination is not. Unclutter your mind and memory so you can open your heart and let your imagination run free; create more agreeable and positive actions – those actions that will take you to your soul's purpose and a fulfilled life.

WRITE A LIST WITH YOUR PASSIONS

Without passion it is difficult to do anything valuable; something that can make a positive impact in your life, on those around you and in the world. Passion is one of the most important ingredients in your journey. Find your passion, find what you love to do, even if you have to do it for free for the rest of your life. If you are doing something now that you are not passionate about, my friend, let me tell you that you are wasting your time.

When you're doing something from your heart with love and kindness, you're supported by your passion, and this is what makes the big difference. So, before you go and change your job or spend money going to university, ask first **what am I passionate about?** Ask yourself who you want to become like. Who are your idols, mentors or the people you admire, look up to and respect the most? You don't need to pick a single person. You may really respect nurses or doctors or firemen or teachers or researchers, scientists, artists or poets. Find those who have similar passions. You should be passionate about everything you do otherwise there's no point to doing it. You can never do your best work, be brilliant and shine if you have no passion for life.

Now I invite you to write ten things that you are passionate about. You can write more than ten or less.

Here are some examples from my list. I'm passionate about:
• personal and professional development
• travelling
• goals and achievements
• fun and relaxation
• human mental and spiritual growth
• coaching, training and teaching

Now, it's your turn. Good luck!

1. _____   2. _____

3. _____   4. _____

5. _____   6. _____

7. _____   8. _____

9. _____   10. _____

Your dreams and passions may be clearer for you, but this is just the beginning. The hard work starts now. Once you have all your passions in front of you, start to decide which ones are most relevant for you to begin working on today. This should become part of your lifestyle. You may never have to work for anyone else again, but if you can't quit your job right now and make a living using whatever it is you're passionate about, do whatever you feel in love with as much as you can and eventually this thing you're passionate about will become your way of life.

This is the secret of happiness and fulfilment. You want to always go in that direction, putting as much energy into it as you can. The more you focus on your chosen passion, the faster it will manifest into a living reality. This is just the beginning, my friend. Step by step, from now forward, you will start to build your life and soul purpose. From now on, every single day of your life will have a new meaning and you will do everything for a reason. You will start to live your life on your terms.

I recommend you don't quit your job until you feel confident enough that you've arrived at the level where you can live and make money just from this, without the need to work for someone else. But don't take forever. If you want to make this your income, you may have to work longer hours at it, after your regular job is through for the day. If you want to do this as a hobby, that's okay, too. Your passion for your hobby will spill over into every part of your life and you will still be fulfilling your soul!

Welcome to the free spirits' world.

Live your life with passion.

Live your life with your rules and on your own terms.

Let's move on!

WRITE A LIST OF YOUR TALENTS AND SKILLS

Do you have any talents or skills? Many of you will say a flat out NO!

Each of us is born with a talent for something, but it needs to be developed and honed. If you have talent such as singing, painting or drawing, dancing, speech or writing, leading people, or crafting, study everything you can about it and practice.

A skill is something we learn to do. Things like carpentry, writing, organising, building, baking, and many others. Skills and talents often overlap. You can be a skilled baker with a talent for creating new flavours in recipes, or you can be a talented artist with a skill for painting on the sides of buildings. (Believe me when I tell you that takes skill).

So why might you believe you have no talents or skills? Because no one ever recognised them in you and you never gave yourself the chance to recognise them in yourself. You may never have had the opportunity to focus or develop your talents and skills. Now you know you can! You have a great job to do. Take time for yourself and write down all the talents and all the skills that you think you have or have learned, even if those skills and talents are modest. Like this, you become more aware of your potential and you will discover a better version of yourself, a version that will become stronger and more viable as you allow yourself to develop.

Why should you do this? Because it will help you to design yourself, to recreate yourself and your life, and it helps you in the end to find your biggest WHY.

Write a list with your talents and skills. I'll give you my examples:
- I have gained some skill in writing.
- I have a talent for inspiring people.

101

Now, write down your own skills and talents.

1. _____   2. _____

3. _____   4. _____

5. _____   6. _____

7. _____   8. _____

9. _____   10. _____

Now that you know your talents and skills, you may start to feel better and have a more positive outlook.

But it's not enough to know what your skills and talents are. You must start to work on them. If you are talented and you don't use, practice, and hone that talent, you won't be any closer to becoming the person you want to be. You need to practice it as often as possible. Doing research is a strong component to developing a skill or talent, too. Find out what's new in that industry and do your best to grow in that direction! By extension, you're going to make a big difference in every area of your life.

CREATE A NEW VISION OF YOURSELF

This next step will help you to define exactly what you want to do and who you want to become. The exercises you've done up to this point should have helped you to understand who you are at the core. Now you will do an exercise that will help you put everything together to give shape to your mission. We will work now on your VISION. You need to know **where** you want to go and **who** or **what** you want to become.

The more you can see and visualise your future self, the more you can grow and get there. To create a vision of yourself and your future, this is the best exercise you can do! It will give you the power and the determination to overcome any obstacle in your life.

In the Bible, it is said that people without vision will perish. If this very old book says that, it seems to me that this is a life principle that has been around for thousands of years. Keep your soul alive and shine by defining your vision.

So, how do you create this vision? Which is the best strategy for doing it? I will share with you the tools that I used to help me get there.

One of the most powerful things you can do is create a vision board with pictures about what you want to achieve and who you want to become. Why with pictures? Because our brain uses images to reinforce ideas. It's one of the ways it connects to your reasoning mind and understands your intention. And after you create your vision board, which should be about what you intend for your future, you can do other exercises along the same line. Create other vision boards, just like the dream boards you created earlier. The difference between the dream bord and vision bord is: the dream board will help you to move forward and will give you motivation to make things happen every day whilst the vision board will give more clarity about yourself as a person, a vision about yourself in and your journey here in life. The vision board is not so much about accomplishment but about clarity and focus. You should make as many boards as you feel it will take to fit all the images and words you want to express. Put your vision boards somewhere you will see them every single day. You want to do this because your unconscious mind will continue to work on the things it has seen and you will start to act and make them happen.

As your visions start to manifest into your reality, you can update your boards to create new visions for yourself. Anyone who wants to succeed in life needs a vision for their future self, with their plans, goals, and dreams to better understand their current life and the direction they want to go; their biggest WHY.

We are almost there…

I remember myself in the middle of the night writing my life purpose and trying to figure out what I wanted to do and who I wanted to become. I was so enthusiastic and excited about it that I couldn't sleep. I wrote down everything like you are doing now, and I had in front of my eyes a lot of pages with my talents, passions, dreams, and goals. I started to put them all together and to find the link between them to understand my MISSION. And guess what? I did it! Around 3 am, I remember I was in Rome, Italy, in the hostel room at the time and that night I felt like the happiest person on the planet just because I understood WHO I am and WHY I am here. I felt guided to create my mission and soul purpose. It's personal and because I consider you my best friend I want to share it with you:

"My SOUL purpose is to inspire and motivate YOU to fight for your DREAMS, to follow your PASSION and to believe in YOURSELF and to help and serve YOU to understand WHO you are and WHY you are here."

Now you know my biggest **WHY** in this life.

I don't know what season your life is in now or where you are, but I know that you want to know who you are and why you are here. I invite you to check everything that you wrote and put it all together to find some common denominator. Now create your own mission statement for your own soul's purpose.

We have slowly arrived at the end of the first part of this magical book. I can't believe we've already covered that much. In this first part, I wanted to show you how to stop merely surviving and start living your life! You are here to be brilliant; you are here to shine. For that reason, Part I is about you getting the knowledge, tools and strategies you need to make a difference in your life. I shared with you all that I've learned about how to live and enjoy life and be happy and grateful, even when you don't have anything and when it seems that there are no reasons to be thankful. The secret is to find those reasons every single day.

I remember a lot of days when I was a child with no food and poor living conditions, but I was always optimistic. Train yourself to become an optimistic person. I hope you will start to practice living this way because this is gold for real life. It is information you won't be taught in schools and you may never have anyone tell you this.

Now you know how to convert your bad situations into good ones, how to take over, how to take the necessary steps to oversee your life, and how to take 100% responsibility for making things happen. Now you know how to raise your standards to become a better version of yourself, to live your life with passion, to find your talents, and exactly how to create your vision and mission in life.

You now have all the tools and strategies to start your own journey and to feel alive, to do what you like and become who you want. Read this book as many times as you need to and use it as a handy reference. Each time you read it you will understand something useful for your daily life. This book is your official guide to change and transformation of your life forever.

In the second part of this book we are going to speak about love. What does love mean? Do you know exactly what it is? Do you love someone? Are you feeling love around you? Do you know how to express love? In the next chapters I will answer all these questions and more.

You will discover a new world, a new way to be happy and a new way to live your life as a love messenger, healing others with the power of love.

Thank you for reading me until now.

Let's go for the next level.

Ready?

PART II

LOVE

PART I

LOVE

Chapter 7.

DEFINITION OF LOVE

"Love has nothing to do with what you are expecting to get — only with what you are expecting to give — which is everything."
– Katharine Heptburn

What is LOVE?

Where does it come from?

How do you know when you love and are loved?

Write down in your own words what love means for you. It may be difficult to define, but I believe that every person has one definition of love because we are created by LOVE, through love and with love. And because of its uniqueness, unlike any other emotion, if it can be called an emotion, you will have to dig deep to choose the correct 'scenes' and 'images' in your mind so you can find the right words to express how LOVE is defined for you.

What is Love?
Love to me is

_____

_____

_____

_____

_____

_____

_____

_____

_____

Love doesn't have to do with what is happening in your life or with the others around you, except perhaps in terms of your perspective. LOVE is like electricity; you can't see it, but you can feel the effects of it.

Even electricity, however, can be measured and seen using the right equipment, but LOVE, like all emotions, is felt. Only the effects are seen.

I remember well when I felt heart broken, I felt that nobody loved me because we were virtually alone, my sister and I. When my parents abandoned us in 2004, the first thoughts that came to my mind was **they don't love me, they don't care about me**. I was extremely upset! Can you imagine a young boy, living in a meagre environment to start with, now without the safety net of adult guidance, supervision, and support, however, lean it may have been? And to add to that, I had my younger sister to protect and support. I believe my parents did do me one act of kindness: they waited until they thought I was old enough to take care of and think for the two of us. But then I was mad at the world, at them, at my life and everyone in it. Even myself! This is what misery does to a person. It makes you miserable and it can be difficult to find your way out.

Later on, I understood that their leaving wasn't because they didn't love me. In fact, I was completely wrong at that time. It wasn't about love at all. I didn't even know what love meant but I must have loved them in my childish way, because I don't remember hating them. I may have been confusing love with needs and attachment.

Years and years later, I personally understand what love means for me and I've created my personal definition of love, something anyone can do according to their own worldview. Each will be unique because we are each unique. Our inner world is like a single universe. Only you understand your own inner world, so it's up to you now to try to express, on paper, your definition of love.

Each of us lives and understands love in a different way, but although the face of love may change, its essence never does. So true abiding love – that essence of the thing – is the same for each of us. Our society, family, and all of our experiences have given us a mix of information about love, and many people strive for that idealised version of love they read about in books or have seen on television.

Love cannot be taken, it can only be given. This is something anyone can understand, and generally begins when love is recognised by the giver. When you recognise the fact that you feel love for something, you begin to learn about love. You can only learn what it is by experiencing it.

For many years I thought my parents left me as an orphan because they didn't love me. I thought all my ex-girlfriends broke up with me because they didn't love me anymore. I used to think that all my old friends would cut the connection with me because their love was finished. My friend, let me tell you that now I realise my mind had led me to believe this. But it wasn't true. Can you see how your thinking reflects your experience? Your perspective of what you experience, not the experience itself, is what becomes embedded in your mind and plays over and over again until you begin to believe that perspective must be correct.

But none of those experiences had anything to do with love. I was expecting something and didn't get it or stopped getting it. And that's it. It didn't have anything to do with love because love wasn't present in what I was receiving. I was not receiving love as I expected it to be, and therefore, I could not recognise it if it were in any way there at all.

Love can warm you or burn you depending on what you know or don't know about it. It holds power, for sure, but should never be used to hold or abuse someone who loves you.

Love has nothing to do with distance, age, religion, sex, nationality, or anything else you can think of. It's our intellectual side that tries to interpret its meaning and essence. LOVE is the soul of our existence. If you exist, you are LOVE. If you are alive you can love and be loved in many different ways and by many different people. For our soul, love is like a light from the SUN; it creates and is created by life; it's actually the food your soul needs to stay alive.

Most people think that if they are no longer happy with someone or beautiful things have stopped happening between them that there is no love anymore. Many couples break up because that initial idealised love is gone. Although the face of love may change (it's face being the way you see it), the essence of love itself never does. Loving someone is like a tree growing; it takes time to mature and can go through many changes along the way. Although a loving person may have love in their heart, it must be carefully sown and cultivated for giving to another. Love can literally be created only if you want it to be. Can you see how love can only be given?

We are all connected by true love. Some of us give ourselves more permission to feel than others do, but that doesn't mean love is not present. How many times have you 'fallen in love'? How many times have you told yourself you will never fall in love again (until the next person you fall in love with comes along)?

Why?

Because love is the only force in life that can make anything happen; it's magical. If you believe in the magic of love, magical things will happen in your life. Love is not like other emotions or simple feelings that come and go; love is within you! Love is YOU! So next time, when you speak with someone about love, speak actually about you and that person.

Love is not what your mind has understood and led you to believe from past experiences with love, it's more than that. What you say, think, and experience about love is only your opinion, but there are seven billion people out there and the same number of definitions of love. So next time you meet or fall in love with someone, don't try to make them love you or understand love in the way you would like them to – the way you do. Accept and respect every person's idea of love. Respect one another even if they don't think or live or love like you do.

And now I feel I should ask you again:

WHAT IS LOVE?

Write down your definition of love again and see if it comes out differently this time. Don't just write what you've heard or seen on TV or read in books; write what you **feel** about love; how it makes you feel; connect with your inner voice and listen to your soul. That is real love! Do you really want to love? Do you really want to be loved? Do you want to be and feel free? Then, my friend, start to discover what love really means. I think a true understanding of love cannot come to us until we are willing to open our heart to it and let go of having it all under control.

To really understand the beauty of love, slow down and stop thinking and analysing so much. Learn to feel more, to listen more, to open your heart to others and to live more in the present, the right HERE and right NOW. Unfortunately, most people go through life never really discovering the real magic of love because they never learned to listen with their heart. We're inundated with 'facts' and 'information" and strayed a long way from using 'intuition' and 'the heart' to guide us. We're too 'busy' using our brain to actually listen to what our heart is telling us.

My friend, you don't want to live a life like this. You want to live your life with passion and love no matter how short or long that life is. To understand the power of love, you need to connect truly with yourself and think of all your experiences, what you've learnt, who you've met and what you've done. And step by step, you will begin to feel more love and feel better about giving love. You will understand that you have to let the past go. Don't worry about the future, just focus on the present and what/how you live. How you live your life is what counts, not the past or the future. How you live today, in fact, will actually determine your future.

I want to share with you my personal definition of love. I asked myself **who was it who taught me all about love?** I thought about my life as far back as I could remember and what I discovered is really powerful. .

Initially, I didn't understand how these negative moments and experiences could teach me about love, but with time I got the point. The events were negative to my conscious mind, but were big lessons for my soul. They allowed me to grow and understand the beauty of this life. Don't try to avoid difficult moments in your life; go through them and learn the lessons or blessings they have for you. You will always benefit from them in some way, but you must look for the benefit. Find what possible good any particular experience has for you so you can just enjoy life the way it is! That doesn't mean you should endure every negative experience others cause for you. You will also learn, in time, how to see the lesson in each negative experience and prevent yourself from experiencing such lessons and experiences again.

I want to share with you my definition of love just to inspire you when you need some inspiration, but remember you need to find yours and write it down so you can refer to it for inspiration, too.

For me, love is the only force that is driving us in this life. It is the most important ingredient for everything we want to achieve or be; for me love is the magic of life, a teacher, a guide, a beautiful and sometimes painful tug that regulates all that we are. Without love, we can't exist or be special and we most assuredly cannot be perfect as a human being. Love gives colour and shape to life. Love is the beginning and the end of humanity.

I can write an entire book about love, but I won't do it here! One day, I will write a book just about the power of love. I still want to share with you what I think love is. Even if you are not the happiest person, it doesn't mean that there is no love in your life.

For me LOVE is also bliss, it is innocence, tranquillity, peace, smiles and happiness.

Love is stupidity, excitement, naughty, fun, mysterious, curious and also a bit cranky.

Love is gratitude, appreciation, thankfulness and grace.

Love is beauty, passion, romance, creativity, and simplicity.

Love is support, understanding, doubts and insecurities and, above all, it is about togetherness.

115

Love is hope, inspiration, motivation for our lives and above all – Love is you, me and everyone and everything in our life!

I love what the Bible says about love in Corinthians 13:4-8.

"Love is patient, love is kind. It does not envy, it does not boast, it is not proud. It does not dishonour others, it is not self-seeking, it is not easily angered, it keeps no record of wrongs. Love never fails."

I think that is the real definition of love. I've shared this passage with you because the writer has succinctly put into words what most people could not. This passage opened my eyes and helped me understand more about this mystery we call Love.

You don't need to go to church to understand the meaning of love; you don't need to be Christian to love all the people around you; you don't need to become 'someone else' to love your life. Just be yourself as you are, UNIQUE and SPECIAL.

Now think about how many times you didn't behave in the way that Bible verse suggests. How many times have you thought that you loved someone yet you behaved jealously or selfishly? You now have a clearer idea of what it really means to love. Still, I invite you to think about it and find your own definition, write it down and start to practice it in your life, at work, with family, friends, and all the people around you, and you will see how, when you treat people with love and kindness, everything in your life will change for better. Magical things will happen.

My goal in this chapter was to guide you to understand and find your own definition of love. Now that you have it, we will move on with the following chapter where I will speak with you about self-love.

Are you ready? Let's speak about love, about YOU!

Chapter 8.

SELF-LOVE

"Love yourself first and everything else falls into line. You really have to love yourself to get anything done in this world."
— **Lucille Ball**

You, as much as anybody in the entire universe, deserve your love and affection. If you have enough love for yourself, then you can give it to others. If not, you cannot give something that you don't have.

Many people don't love themselves. They are always finding fault with what they do or who they are. They persist in negative self-talk. They expect love without giving it, but everything in this life works on the principle of the universe: GIVE-RECEIVE. **You get** in equal measure and kind **what you give**. Even if you don't understand this principle, it works in your life. All the principles of the universe are at work, whether we're aware of them or not. If you understand that you get what you give, you can intentionally apply this principle and make more good things happen for you. If you feel as though you're giving and not getting, perhaps you're not being open to receiving love from others or maybe you're expecting love to show itself in some other way, not seeing it for what it is.

For 14 years, I grew up in a family where the notion of LOVE was missing. Self- love was non-existent. There were completely different things, but not this one. I am honest and sincere with you when I tell you I didn't know how to love myself.

When I was 24, I discovered myself and I asked myself a lot of questions about me, about life and about the people around me. I was wondering about falling in love with someone, but I couldn't because I didn't have love for myself. I felt unworthy, unattractive and unimportant. I intellectually understood that you can't give something you don't have, but I didn't understand why I didn't have it to give. I hadn't **experienced** love, that I am lovable.

For many years I lived with pain and suffering in this area until I discovered, with the help of one of my spiritual mentors, a new world with love, light, forgiveness and hope. He told me a person will never change until they suffer enough. You will never understand what love is if you don't experience living without it; you can't appreciate and understand happiness if you don't know what sadness and pain are.

Lastly and perhaps most importantly, before you choose to be with someone else, you must focus on yourself; learn how to live alone and be at peace with yourself. Then you will be able to **choose to be with someone** not because you need to, but because you want to.

I remember during my childhood I always had this fear in my mind that I didn't want to be alone. I felt I needed to always have someone close to me. This was a natural reaction to being abandoned and came from the fact that my parents were not affectionate people; I didn't receive enough love from them to help me to build love for myself.

When my parents left and I had to face real moments alone, with my little sister, all my fears become reality. From that moment, I was always afraid that friends, girlfriends and even my sister would one day abandon me the way my parents had. I had deep trauma and was in true depression. I looked at everything negatively. I lived with this state of mind for many years and I didn't love anyone. I just attached to people because I needed to have someone there. I didn't know how to love them or how to receive love from them. I couldn't recognise love when it was shown to me.

I still keep asking questions, meeting a lot of people, reading books, travelling, and learning new things and little by little I'm starting to understand more about the concept of love. I've been to seminars and courses and I've bought and read books about love because I felt it was missing from my life. Actually it was always there, but I didn't know how to unlock it. Step by step I started to work on myself and build self-love.

This was perhaps the most difficult process I went through to grow in terms of personal development. I didn't have respect for myself either. I didn't see myself as being beautiful. In my mind, I had no potential; what I saw in myself I saw as 'not enough' or 'not good enough'. I had a poor self-image and I felt useless. I couldn't see my meaning or my purpose in this world. All I needed in that moment was to have someone close to me to make me feel secure, but I never really believed they were there because they actually liked me and certainly not because they loved me. I just didn't want to be alone. I was afraid and constantly focused on my fear; the more I focused on it, the greater it became in my mind and the more it influenced my life, my perception of people, and my actions.

Building self-love is a long process and many of us need to work on it. It's the first area you should work on, because without this foundation, you will never have the confidence to realise your potential, and this will extend into all areas of your life. Look at yourself and start to analyse what you see and think you know. Do you like what you see, how you feel, what you have or who you have become? In general, look at where you came from, where you are and where you want to go. Whether you like what you see or not will depend on how much you love yourself.

I wanted to write about this because no one at school or in society is passionate about teaching us how to love ourselves; no one cares about this as a life skill and for that reason many young people are lost; they don't know who they are because they don't have love for themselves; they have low self-esteem and little confidence to become emotionally healthy adults.

HOW CAN YOU LEARN TO LOVE YOURSELF?

There are lots of ways and steps to getting there, but I believe this is one of **the most important**:

Accept the way you are whatever it is and live life by loving the person you are today. You cannot do anything until you accept the way you are, the things you do, and the way you act, react or behave. Only then can you work towards creating a better version of you.

You don't need to continue to live with what you are today. If you don't like the way you behave in certain situations, work to change that. Find someone, real or fictitious, who behaves in a way you admire and strive to emulate their good behaviour. Eventually, that's what you'll become. It will be part of you. Don't misconstrue this as false behaviour or 'trying to be something you're not'. Think like a child who is emulating the good points of their parents' behaviour. There's nothing wrong with learning how to behave from others. This is how we learn everything in life, from each other and the examples of our experience.

When I speak about self-love, I'm not speaking about selfishness or egoism or egocentrism; I'm simply talking about that care and love that you would show for anyone else. Self-love is about seeing the child you are inside and loving that child, caring for who that child is and taking steps to guide him; your soul needs nurturing, and who knows your soul better than you? Care for your body, for your heart, your passions, your talents, your dreams, goals, plans and desires in the same way you would encourage a dear friend with theirs. Care and nurture ALL that YOU are!

I've been through difficult moments in my life, a lot of pain, lots of ups and downs. And through it all I asked God why all this happened to me. What did I do to deserve this? Why do I have to pass this 'test'? And I used to fight with and provoke God to give me signs that He existed. In the end I understood why I needed to suffer through so many times. For me, this was the way to learn to love myself. For others, there may be different ways, and for all of us there are special lessons that we need to learn to be able to feel something beautiful in us.

I had the wrong idea about love; I was confusing love with others' feelings because I wasn't happy with myself and my life. But everything started to change when I became aware of real love for myself and for others. I see all around me people who don't love their body, they don't like the way they look, they don't care what they eat, the way they live or what they read. I used to do the same. I was disrespectful with myself until I discovered how beautiful and unique I am, and from that moment, everything changed like a miracle. No more smoking, no more alcohol, no more negative gossip, no more blame, no more complaining, no more procrastination, and best of all, no more fear.

FEAR ENDS WHERE LOVE STARTS

I only began to understand this when I started to change my habits and train myself to care. I started to be grateful, to eat healthily, to go for treatments for my body, to attend different events for my soul and to go to the cinema for fun; I started to read books and I stopped watching TV. This one was, for me, one of the most difficult habits to change and

121

honestly I was only able to change it by substituting it with one of the most powerful things I practice: READING BOOKS.

I just gave you an example from my personal life of how I discovered love for myself. You will start to feel love for yourself and you will change your FOCUS from outside to inside when you get it into your head that you can be lovable, you can be loved in the same way you can care for and love others. For example, if you are a woman, you will stop wanting to be like a top model. You will stop comparing yourself to them. You can still be inspired by them, but you don't have to look like them. Or if you are a man, you would stop looking at professional athletes with a desire to be like them. (Of course there is the exception to the rule. If you truly aspire to be a top model or a professional athlete, then those people can be your mentors and you will do the work to get yourself there).

Focus more on you and the way you live **your** life; stop comparing yourself with millionaires. Everyone is here for a special reason and you need to find, accept and work on your unique potential and purpose. Each of us is unique in our own beautiful way. Believe me when I tell you that millionaires, athletes and professional models all have their own sets of doubts about themselves and their abilities.

Let me tell you something my friend, you can have all the money in the world and you can be the most beautiful and famous one, but nothing will change for you because happiness needs to come from your heart. It's something you can't buy, though many try; you can't make it, you can only nurture what is inside you, no matter your social or physical condition. Happiness and fulfilment come in the same packet as self-love. When you find a way to love and respect yourself, to appreciate who you are and what are you doing, then you will be happy and fulfilled.

I want to share with you my **7 steps to learning how to discover self-love.** These are the steps that helped me to become free and happy and to feel love for myself. Whatever you do, if there is not love, you will feel empty.

STEP 1: ACCEPT YOURSELF

This is the step that will unlock all your feelings and emotions about yourself. This is the most important step in this journey because in no way can you discover love if you don't know who you are. Sounds cliché, right? But you'd probably be surprised to learn that, judging by the condition of the world at large, most people are not in touch with their inner love.

Nothing can happen if you don't know and accept **who** you are. **Who** will be defined by you, your character, the way you act and live and therefore only you can define who you are. Because you have this power, you can make changes in you, and there will be a lot of dealing with your worst enemy – your mind and its subconscious and unconscious directors. But you **can** change. Just remember that perception is everything. What you see is not only what you get, but what you give. Those things you repeat every day become you and your life.

Don't start looking around for ways to love yourself. Although there are many strategies to learn this art, to step back to the experiences that inform who you are today, it goes much deeper than techniques. You need to change your beliefs about **you** and **your personal reality**. YOU are the one who stops you from feeling love for yourself. I'm not talking about being self-centred, I talking about the way you feel about yourself, about who you perceive yourself to be.

Let me give you some examples of the beliefs I had before I started to change and feel something good and positive about myself.

"I am not beautiful." I actually looked in the mirror and believed that what I was looking at was not attractive in any way; there was no way I am good enough to even be out in public because people will stare at me. "I am not beautiful."

"I don't have enough." I actually had no idea as to what I wanted to be or have enough of, or what enough actually was, but I also had no standards by which to know this. All I knew was that I must be lacking in anything that matters and even those that don't matter. I never put words to this feeling, such as I don't have enough skill; I don't have enough brains, I don't have enough training, or I don't have enough experience. I believed I was unimportant, a ghost in society, incapable of being paid attention to because "I don't have enough."

"I can't do, (and therefore I can't be)." I was unable to understand the concept of **wisdom comes with experience**, because I'd never heard it or had it explained to me. I had to learn it on my own and, of course, this took years. But back then, I believed I had no worth to anyone because I really couldn't do anything. I didn't quite get that **I couldn't do anything because I hadn't learned anything**. Fortunately, I was able to make the change later and design my life rather than following it randomly.

But back then I was always looking out for someone else first; I was always the last one on my list because subconsciously I didn't believe I was worth anyone spending any time with, including myself. So I was constantly reaching out, giving and doing for others in the mistaken belief that this was the only way I would have someone around me all the time; the only way I would feel some kind of acceptance.

It was only when I started to redirect my focus from the external environment of seeking approval to the internal one of seeking self-love that everything started to change.

When I talk about 'internal environment', I'm including the heart / gut / physical environment and the mind / brain / consciousness environment together.

So how do you do this? How do you connect with the internal self in order to make changes?

It's important to first understand how the human mind works.

If you're willing to give up old resentments and outmoded techniques for living that haven't worked for you in the past and take on this journey, you can master your life.

Those who are successful in mastering the art of self-healing possess one thing: the experience and knowledge of universal laws: how the universe works. Specifically, what stands between you and your future successes is what you believe to be true about yourself and the world in which you live. We all become the laws and notions we believe in.

These cutting edge principles are timeless natural laws. They will compel you to take action and they require passion. The laws which govern consciousness, humanity, and the universe do not waver. They're working whether you're aware of them or not, but without focused intent, they may be working against you.

The transformational change you enact will be the result of your artful exploration and personal evolution. Instead of **being yourself**, you will **create yourself**.

One of the hardest things for me to change was my belief about my appearance. I believed that I was not beautiful or tall enough. So every day I would look at myself in the mirror and repeat, **"I'm so beautiful,"** even though I didn't believe it. I did this for at least two weeks, until I decided it was just empty words. I looked in the mirror that day, quietly studying my face, my hair, my ears and eyes, everything I could see. I looked deep into my own eyes and saw the person inside, the person only I knew, and in that moment, I loved him. I loved that person. I actually felt an emotion that seemed to be a combination of joys supported by an undertone of wisdom.

We all have that innate wisdom in us. There is really nothing to 'work at loving'. When you feel it, you will know it. There are no words to be put to it.

In that moment I started to see myself as I really am, on the inside. My opinion of what I saw of myself on the outside now suddenly didn't seem all that bad. As days went by, I experienced more and more of the kindness within me until I knew I was beautiful.

Accepting what is allows us to see its beauty.

You can also do this through meditation or you can simply lie on your back or sit in a comfortable position, without distractions. Turn off your cell phone. Wait for a time when you can be assured of privacy.

Close your eyes and relax. Take a few slow deep breaths in and out through your nose. Try to keep any distracting images from your mind (cars outside, TV shows that replay in your mind, your work schedule). You want to envision any other scene from your life, anything at all that passes through, beginning from the moment you closed

You can do what I did and simply use the mirror to look into the windows of your soul. This worked for me because I was dealing with the issue of physical appearance. But the above exercise can be very revealing, regardless of where you stand in your personal evolution, and it's something that can be continued throughout your lifetime.

Whatever you want to change in your life, accept it first, see it for what it is and then you can change it much more easily. There is nothing that you can't do.

So the first step to self-love is to **accept yourself**.

Let's go for the second one, which is equally important. Are you ready?

STEP 2: FORGIVE YOURSELF

Humans, as far as we know, are the only species who espouse the concept of forgiveness. It's often difficult to forgive and sometimes seemingly impossible to forgive ourselves. The exercise in STEP 1 will help you to forgive many of those whom you felt wronged by in the past. But forgiveness cannot always be about clearing our past.

Think about how many times you did something and you couldn't forgive yourself. There may be things even today that are hidden in your psyche, buried. But remember, universal law is always working. If you have a history of taking blame or being the scapegoat, you may be unconsciously blaming yourself for things over which you had no real control. You may be holding onto imagined hurts when everyone else has forgotten about them.

One of the downsides of taking responsibility for our actions is beating ourselves too much for the mistakes we may have made while learning and growing. You have to accept your humanness. Humans are not perfect and you will make mistakes all the time, even if you do learn from them. Still, you have to accept those mistakes in the same way you must accept everything else about yourself before you can truly love yourself. You need to be patient with yourself and give yourself time; practice forgiveness for the small things and when the big ones come along, it will be easier to forgive them. If you want to feel more love, part of the secret is forgiving others and yourself.

I know this is really hard sometimes. I remember when I first started this process, I thought that I wouldn't make it. I hadn't yet learned to forgive myself for anything. I grew up in a family environment where I was blamed for everything that happened in the family. I was never shown any forgiveness, kindness or understanding. I just always felt bad, like having no food or money was somehow really my fault. But I was made to feel that way and the idea of this **became my experience**, one which stayed with me and continued to replay itself long after I'd left the orphanage.

I always felt like I was carrying something really heavy on my shoulders and my back. What I believed about myself had literally manifested itself physically into a stooped appearance. But I sensed something in me that wanted to fly; to feel so light and to be free. Now I understand that I was keeping myself in my own prison and most people do the same. I set myself free from this prison and I learnt how to forgive myself for anything I'd ever done or was unable to do. For those people who laid blame on me for things I never did, I forgave them.

It took me years to arrive where I am today, happy and enjoying my life. When I make a mistake, I forgive myself immediately. I understand it's all a normal part of this amazing journey called life. When you start to work on this, step by step you will start to realise that you feel much better mentally and emotionally and this will translate into better physical health as well. You will understand more about your potential and how you can shine and be brilliant even when you don't know something perfectly well, even when you're still making mistakes. At the same time, you'll start to feel much love and appreciation for yourself. And the more you feel love for yourself, the more you can give it away to others to help them and inspire them to grow and travel better in their journey. You will begin to reflect the world around you now in a positive way. Everything you give is received, giving the receiver more to give, which returns to you. In other words, give love = get love. Give negativity = build negativity. Teach and inspire = learn and be inspired.

The second step to self-love is to **forgive yourself**.

Let's discover now the next step that allows you to understand more about the concept of self-love.

Ready?

STEP 3: PROTECT YOURSELF

What does it really mean to protect yourself? Everyone needs some kind of protection, but this may be a new concept for you even though you've very likely already been protecting yourself in a number of ways.

One of the reasons that you may not feel love for yourself is because you don't know how to protect yourself from others who may act against you, blame you or stop you in some way. Learning to protect yourself is part of self-love.

One day when I arrived home from school, happy in the way kids are without any rational reason to be so, I heard my mother and father fighting and complaining about our financial and material situation. I was just ten years old, but mature enough to understand that something was not going well. I didn't know exactly what that was, but I had a feeling that soon something was going to happen. In fact, that very same day my mother came to me and told me she wanted to speak to me about something serious. She apologised first. Then with tears in her eyes, she tried to explain to me that my father couldn't work anymore. He was unable to provide money and there was not enough for us to survive on. He had been buying alcohol and drinking every day. He was an alcoholic and he didn't care that much about our family. I was listening to my mother really carefully and I didn't know exactly what she wanted from me. She tried to excuse herself because she felt sick and she was complaining about my father. She tried to pass him the responsibility of telling me whatever it was she was trying to tell me, but he wasn't even aware of anything that was going on around him.

I still didn't get the point my mother was trying to make. In the end she just told me directly. Someone needed to go to work and bring money and food into the home for the entire my family. And like my mother, I seriously thought that someone needed to care about this. It was a huge priority now. Innocently, I asked my mother who the person was who would be going to work to provide money and bring food home. She didn't answer me at first. After a few seconds of silence, she looked in my big eyes and said, "YOU! It's your turn now. We did a lot for you and now you have to go to work and help us."

"I can't!" I replied to her. I didn't understand in the beginning what that was supposed to mean, and I asked my mother how I can do this if I'm going to school.

And her words just made me cry when she told me I would have to leave school to go to work. "You can't go to school anymore."

I didn't know how to react and because I loved my family so much, I just did it without giving it a second thought! The hard part started when I saw my colleagues coming from school and they were free and smiling and happy and I was alone with animals and plants working in a factory all day to make a living to support my family.

At that point, I began crying and questioning everything. Why was this happening to me? What did I do wrong to deserve this? Why can't I go to school anymore? Why do I need to do this? There were lots of questions every day in my mind. I started to suffer a lot mentally and I felt so much emotional pain. The only moment I was happy was when I arrived at home and my sister told me about her day at school. I was so happy to bring her some food and support her in any way I could.

After many years I understood that I didn't know how to protect myself back then, how to follow what I wanted and I couldn't say anything about it.

The reason that I shared this short part of my personal story with you is to make you understand that you need to learn how to protect your SOUL, your DREAMS, your PASSION, what you really love to do and who you really want to become. Children are almost always put into this kind of situation, where they can't defend themselves, their ideas, their wants and their needs. As an adult, now, you need to be aware of this and not allow anyone to interfere or come between you and your life journey. At the same time, if you have children in your life, you need to recognise that they have hearts and minds, too, just like you do. Give them the space to express their desires and protect them against irrational scolding or oppression.

Pay attention and learn how to protect yourself spiritually and energetically, not just materially and physically. This is important, but it's not the most important! YOU need to follow your heart and protect yourself and you will discover the magic of self-love.

The third step to self-love is to **protect yourself**.

I hope you will learn from my mistakes and my story. Let's go to the next step on the journey to discovering more about self-love.

STEP 4: BE PATIENT

Being patient is one of the most powerful virtues that human beings can practice. A lack of patience is really common today. People are anxious and in a hurry all the time. We get nervous when the train or bus is late and we don't like to wait in the queue, we don't like it if someone is a bit slow to understand something and we want everything to happen quickly so we can get on with our day. We're forced to stick to timetables. Over time we may get lost just doing 'stuff that needs to be done' in a day or a week. Technology and modern society along with all the systems that are trying to influence us every day have cost us our ability to be patient.

In this session I want to speak about the patience you must build in yourself so you can accept any mistakes you make along life's journey. By being patient, you can observe your mistakes, correct and learn from them, as you continue to record in your journal and improve your methods. Always allow that you are not perfect and neither is anyone else.

The human mind works like a data base. It calculates what we do and how many times we do it, then it prioritises them. You end up with that, but you can change it because you were the original programmer. You can change it to be something else. This takes patience.

When you learn patience for yourself and others, you will start to feel more self-love. When you become more patient and let things go, when you stop trying or needing to be in control of everything, and when you slow down and refocus your energy and attention more on yourself rather than on other people, you create more time and space to discover your own mind and ways. You will start to love more about yourself, who you are and the way you are. Remember, it's all about perception and projection – how you see yourself and the image you want to project. For that reason it's really important to take responsibility for your thoughts – make them worthwhile! Make them work **for** you!

Start being nicer, kinder, and friendlier with yourself every single day. Go easy on yourself in the same way you would for a friend. And wherever you are – at work, out with friends, home with family, passing someone casually on the street – it doesn't matter. Your behaviour should be the same in all situations. Remember to be patient with yourself daily.

The fourth step to self-love is to **be patient**.

Each step builds upon and therefore becomes more powerful than the previous step. The next step is one of my favourites.

STEP 5: BE GRATEFUL

Years ago, I didn't know anything about gratitude. I used to pray from time to time, though I do not consider myself a religious person. I never had a certain ritual of going to church. I appreciate and respect people who do, but for myself, I only went from time to time and to different churches. I don't want to get into religion because actually I don't follow any of the traditional world religions; I've built my own philosophy of life, and for me, LOVE is the best religion. It can understand and be tolerant of all others. Maybe in another book I will speak about it, but now I want to stay focused on self-love, and being grateful will help you to unlock a lot of your feelings about yourself and how you view your world.

I started understanding the concept of gratitude more than five years ago. I had read many books on the subject and understood the principle and the universal Law of Gratitude, so in the beginning, I used to openly speak thanks for my blessings on a daily basis, as a habitude. I had in my mind that I needed to do this, and after a while I started to do it with feeling because I found I liked doing it and the way it made me feel. I loved that feeling; it was almost magical how powerful I felt.

Being grateful will help you understand your own attitude toward the things you have and the blessings you're receiving. You'll understand more about yourself, what makes you happy and why; why you might become nervous, anxious, sad, frustrated and so on. It will help you to connect with what's important to you, the real you, not the cheap façade you may have been putting on to make others think you're okay, doing fine, just wonderful! And the most important thing is it will help you to live in the present, HERE and NOW, because each time you express gratitude for something, you are in touch with you inner self.

Nowadays, every morning I have a portion in my personal journal where I write all the reasons I am grateful for that day. This helps me to feel my emotions and to understand where they come from. I can tell you that the habitude of gratitude will change your life forever. The most important thing is that you can't be negative when you are grateful. You can try, but it just won't work. When you are grateful, negativity cannot show up.

So I developed a very good attitude of being positive all the time, no matter what. This was so powerful that I found I was no longer blaming and complaining. Instead, I was focusing more on things that I have and who I am. I started, little by little, to love more and appreciate more and to be gentler with myself.

Start writing, every day, 3 things you are grateful for in that day and do it for 30 days. You will see how powerful it is, how much better you will feel about yourself and about life in general. You will start to be grateful for big things and small things, whether it's some unexpected cash or someone holding the door open for you when your arms are full of groceries. You will begin to truly understand the meaning of life, and that for each of us life means something different.

Being grateful will bring more prosperity and positivity into your life as well. You will experience having more energy and more vitality, more love and more passion. So what are you waiting for? Start today and write down some reasons you are grateful or things you are grateful for. Then start to work on the habitude of gratitude. Practice being grateful for every turn of events, every little thing, expected or unexpected, and everything you are able to create in your life. Remember if you want to have something that you never had, you need to do something that you never did.

The fifth step to self-love is to **express gratitude**.

Let's keep going!

STEP 6: KEEP A JOURNAL

When I first heard about keeping a personal journal, I actually started to laugh. I thought, "No, I can't do that, I'm not a high school girl." I was actually sceptical about this because I couldn't understand how it could possibly benefit me.

One day I'd been to a seminar with one of my favourite mentors, and in between other things he spoke about the power of keeping a journal. In that moment I thought, "NO, this can't be real! Even he's speaking about that; this is too much!"

But after that seminar I promised myself that if this was something that would help me grow, I would do some research to find out the alleged miracle of keeping a personal journal.

And so I did!

What I discovered literally amazed me, and from that very day I started to keep one, not a proper one, but at least I had gotten started with a little pocket journal where I started to write things. At first nothing happened and I felt a bit down. I was expecting to see the miracle and the power of this journal, but at that time, I couldn't see anything.

Eventually I finished one, two, three journals, and every time I finished one, I was both excited and melancholic. I started to use bigger and bigger books and I read whatever I could about journaling, looking for details about how to properly keep one. And now, after 3 years, I'm mastering it. I'm writing every single day with more passion and elaboration and detail and gratitude.

One of the most beautiful things about journaling is that it helped me when I felt alone, when I wanted to speak with someone and no one was around to pour my thoughts into, when I had a victory or failure, and pretty much any time I just needed to express myself. I developed my own style of writing, and now I actually just follow my heart. I write whatever I feel I need to put down on the paper without censorship or editing words in my head as I go.

Exercise: When you begin journaling, practice what's referred to as 'free writing'. It's a technique in which you will write continuously without worrying about spelling or grammar or even topic. When you read it back, some of it won't make sense, but you will be able to break mental blocks and reveal what's really going on in your mind. The idea is to write without any self-criticism and just let your mind go. You can put down anything you want to write about. Just let the words come out. Step away, then go back and read your free writing in a few days.

You will then see yourself and your thoughts differently. When you write this way, your mind is connected with your heart. You are allowing yourself to become even more creative and sensitive, more perceptive and more aware about how you view your reality.

The power of keeping a journal really works. I only discovered this by doing it; by practicing it every day for more than a 1000 days in a row.

You may be thinking: **Where is the link with self-love?**

This is the part I love most. Every single person who starts a personal journal does so after they really understand the meaning of their life, and more so when they realise their life is important. This is actually when they start to feel love for themselves. When I write in my diary, I feel so much love for myself and I feel I care and treat myself with kindness.

You will develop self-love once you start to keep a journal, and I recommend you start today. Your life is important, your life is beautiful, don't waste it, record it, live it, enjoy it!

So how do you start?

136

Simple!

You just start to write. From the moment you wake up, think about what makes you happy. You can write in the morning or at night or whenever you have time. It's best to set aside a certain time of day for this and you will begin to look forward to it. I usually write how I feel that day, who I've met, what I did, what I learnt, what I am grateful for, and sometimes my inner thoughts, those thoughts that I usually don't share with anyone. The more you write the more you will discover yourself and the better you will feel. You'll recognize the good about yourself, you'll feel much more love, particularly self-love, much more appreciation, and more self-esteem. Writing in a journal is a strong component to self-discovery; every single human being should have one!

What are you waiting for?

Start today to write your life story. You are in charge of it, do it in any way you like. Over the years, you will be delighted to reread them and see the directions your life has taken.

The sixth step to self-love is to **keep a journal**.

This was one of my favourite steps, but we move now to the last one and absolutely one of the most powerful.

STEP 7: PRACTICE MEDITATION

Maybe meditation is something new for you, or perhaps you already know something about it. For me, it was something I discovered and literally fell in love with a few years ago. I wrongly believed I couldn't do it, that it was not for me. I believed I wasn't all that spiritual and that meditation was reserved for monks and gurus who sat on mountaintops contemplating the universe and all of its mysteries.

I remember, almost two years ago, like it was yesterday, I was alone back in my box room in London, and before I went to sleep I used to pray or just stay in silence. I was, in fact, already practicing a form of meditation although I didn't know it. One day I realised most of my mentors and friends practiced meditation and I was curious to understand why; what were benefits they were receiving from it? I told myself **why not try something new if it's so trendy now**.

I didn't know how to do it, so I found something on YouTube to guide me through. In the first week, I fell asleep within 5 minutes of starting the meditation, so I stopped doing it for a while. But I learned how to stay awake during my meditation sessions and slowly I was able to master it. Now I can meditate up to 30 minutes at a time, but usually average ten minutes daily.

I can imagine some your questions now:

What is the connection between meditation and self-love?
And why should I do that?

First, let's talk about what meditation is.

By definition, meditation is simply the act of focusing deeply, in silence, as a method of relaxing the mind so as to 'get in touch' with inner consciousness, thereby leading to self-discovery, self-renewal and spiritual growth.

Traditional meditation often involves a spiritual component. Those who have been practicing it for many years are beyond any self-indulgence, learning self-love or contemplating daily encounters. Their goal is to connect with the mind of God and the Universe, to understand and be one with all things.

You may wish to take this far, or you may only want to use meditation as a means of getting in touch with your own consciousness and how it plays a part in your behaviour, the way you view yourself and your world. The patterns your mind has set up for you can more easily be changed when you learn to meditate deeply.

When you're deep in meditation, you have the opportunity to connect with that part of yourself that is overshadowed during daily waking hours, when everything is about time schedules and the hustle and bustle of everyday activities. You are in silence, within and without; you feel any emotion that arises.

Learning to meditate is simple.

Choose a time when you can sit quietly for a designated period, when you will not be disturbed or distracted.

- Sit quietly in a relaxed position. Be sure you aren't so comfortable that you fall asleep! An upright chair works well, or you can sit on a mat or towel on the floor with your back straight.
- Cross your legs or extend them in a relaxed position. Your hands and arms can fall at your side or you can rest them on your thighs or knees.
- Close your eyes and take a few deep breaths in and out through your nose. Envision a place between your eyebrows. This is where the legendary 'third eye' is located. Focus on this spot.
- You will hear outside noises, such as a car passing. Let it pass and return your focus to your breathing. Give a visual component to your breath. Assign it a colour and watch it move smoothly into your nose, filling your lungs, and then moving freely out through your nose.

As you begin to relax, do not think about anything in particular. Your objective is to relax and 'see' the inner workings of your subconscious mind. Remain in the moment; don't let your mind wander.

The process of meditation follows a particular order. By following your breath, you will get into a rhythm that supports a relaxed mind. The mind is cleared, the body and mind are relaxed, and the focus in inward, to the consciousness, not on the external world. When you reach a state of contemplation where you are no longer distracted by what's outside you, your meditation will deepen.

You will experience more positivity and love in your life because you are able to give more of those, and the more you meditate the more you will discover yourself. You will feel much more love for who you are and what you're doing.

Meditation is like a medication; actually it's better to meditate than to medicate in many instances. Other benefits of meditation are enhanced creativity, keener intuition, deeper sleep, heightened awareness, lower blood pressure, better grade scores, greater insight, and general well-being. With continued practice, you will start to see progressively greater results in your personal and professional life.

Most people limit themselves. They frown on meditation as being some Eastern religion which might interfere with their own religious practices. But meditating is free and completely personal, and it's for everyone, no matter what your general religious beliefs.

But what's the real point? You can relax when you're sleeping, right?

When you're asleep, you're not consciously aware of what's going on around you. Only someone who is highly advanced can control their dreams in order to exact change or understand their meaning. During meditation, you are conscious and awake, aware of your surroundings but able to 'tune them out'. You can, with enough practice, focus your subconscious mind on your cells, your physicality, your DNA, and in this way, you can even heal your body. Because of this heightened awareness, the subconscious takes its cue to make the change you are focused on, and in a short time, it will begin to carry over to your normal everyday state of mind. It will see this as a projection of what you are and will be reinforced each time you go deep into meditation.

You will be more aware about almost everything, and you will grow spiritually and personally.

Meditation is a great solution for people with low self-esteem and for people who haven't learned to love and accept themselves mentally or physically. Meditation can take you on a beautiful journey that will help you to live your life on your terms. It will take you out of your comfort zone and allow you to grow every single day while it reinforces only the good messages you put into your subconscious while you meditate. Be aware that some painful memories may come up at first; see them for what they were and change your perspective of them in your mind. Once you clear up painful memories, your positive changes will grow exponentially.

Practicing meditation every day helps you learn how to listen to your body and control that part of your subconscious mind that's been telling you there's something wrong with you. When you meditate, the focus is on your inner self and not on the environment. Practice meditation every day for about 5-10 minutes or more if you can as a means of relaxing, learning about yourself and your behaviours, and retraining your subconscious to relay positive messages during your day. In this way, you can enjoy life more.

Chapter 9.

UNCONDITIONAL LOVE

"The greatest gift that you can give to someone is the gift of unconditional love and acceptance."
– Brian Tracy

What does 'unconditional love' really mean?

From the time we're old enough to understand language, we're bribed with toys or sweets to make us stop crying. No one wants to deal with a crying child. In fact, most adults don't know **how** to deal with crying, even if another adult is doing the crying.

From an early age, we're shown what appears to be love; we're cooed at, given a pat on the shoulder, talked at and sometimes even scolded. The reality of these actions is that they are merely a means of trying to make us conform to whatever it is our parents or guardians or friends need from us. They need us to stop crying, stop craving and stop wanting them to show us the affection that has been drummed out of **them** since **they** were children.

I remember when I was at school my colleagues often had something new to play with and I would ask them where these things came from.

"From my parents because I have been good at school," they would answer. "They told me if I am good at school, than they will send me on holiday", "if you don't miss a day of school, I will buy you a new pair of shoes", "if you do not cry anymore I will buy you that lollipop".

We might look back and see this limited mentality as funny, but it has actually been stunting the spiritual and intellectual growth of humans across the board.

So what's the solution? The alternative?

The alternative is to show unconditional love to our children and to the adults in our lives who can then show it to others.

Why is it so important to discover unconditional love?

People don't have unconditional love for others because they don't have it for themselves.

- They have never learned to forgive themselves for all the real or imagined slights they see themselves responsible for.
- They are afraid to show real emotions because they feel that doing so will somehow diminish them.
- They fear becoming vulnerable to further hurts.
- They have worked very hard to cover their feelings, creating a necessary mask that gets them through the day.
- They are the victims of learned behaviours; they believe that not crying or being overly emotional will make them more likeable.
- Women in particular, who are more prone to crying than men, have been repeatedly chastised for doing so, thereby invalidating their feelings.

- Children learn that when they cry, they will receive sweets or toys, and they will learn to use that to their gain but when they are really in need of love, their crying is viewed as a mere annoyance and is not taken seriously.

Nowadays, it's difficult to find real love in any kind of relationship. Most of the time, although we're looking for love, we settle for what appears to be the safety of a relationship. Why? Because this is how we were raised.

"If you do this, I will give you this." But this trade-off is a poor substitution for real love founded on mutual respect, admiration and common ground. Too many couples stay in relationships because they just don't want to be alone, but this will only result in a relationship of convenience.

"I will love you if you are this or that, if you do this or that, only if you behave a certain way or have enough money or dress well." This places conditions on that love, which is not real love. It removes love when the conditions are no longer met. It is the opposite of unconditional love.

Think about your relationships with your spouse, children, parents, and friends. Are you loving someone unconditionally? Are you accepting someone the way they are? Are you able to live your life and love people without any conditions being placed upon them?

Unconditional love places no limits, conditions or excuses on another person in return for that love.

As you allow yourself to think and feel like this, you may find that loving others unconditionally is easier than loving yourself that way. It may be difficult for you to do because you will have to draw up all the old resentments and hurts of the past and clear them out. But it's worthy and beautiful to discover that you are enough just as you are. It's a powerful feeling to love yourself as a human being and accept yourself as you are, without any need for approval or results that others want from you. You don't need to show anything to anyone. Just be! Just enjoy life and discover the magic of unconditional love.

Most of us use the word love wrongly. I believe that real and true love is pure, is something magical, and has nothing to do with qualification. It's about others. By that I mean I believe that unconditional love is happening when you care for others, when you are interested in other people's happiness, but not at the expense of sacrificing your love for yourself. I like to say that unconditional love is like pure water from the mountain river; whether you like it or not, accept it or not, it's there, and regardless of what you do, you can't stop it!

Personally, I discovered unconditional love for people, nature, animals and the planet itself because of my experiences in life. I was really sceptical that something like that existed. I suffered a lot emotionally and many times I was broken hearted, with tears in my eyes, disappointed, sad and going through a lot of emotional and physical pain. I didn't understand at that moment why life put me in the position I was in – living through all of these painful and challenging situations. I kept asking **why me? What have I done to deserve this? If God exists somewhere in the universe, why allow me to live this?** And the beautiful part came after I learned that our challenges are never too much for us. We are here to learn and we are given the experiences we need to do so.

In time, I understood that I actually needed to pass through all of that to be able and to grow enough to understand the power of unconditional love.

Now stop reading and ask yourself: How many times have I:

- Felt loved?
- Really loved someone unconditionally?
- Cared about strangers?
- Felt unconditional love for myself?

- Shared or offered my resources, knowledge and possessions with others?
- Volunteered to help someone I didn't know?
- Thought to add value to the world without asking anything in exchange?
- Given compliments away without expecting to receive one back?
- Given answers without expecting any reward?

And now you can continue the list by yourself, because the list is long.

How many times have I…

My friend, I want to make it clear that unconditional love has nothing to do with romantic love, although they are not mutually exclusive. Romantic love should also be unconditional, but unconditional love is not necessarily romantic love. The highest level of mature love is unconditional, but it's rarely found and unlikely that somebody explained it, taught it or demonstrated it to you.

Start to train yourself to discover more, to practice more and of course to believe and experience more unconditional love for others and yourself. Begin with your spouse or children.

Unconditional love is not a feeling. It's an action that you must decide to take. It's a decision to accept someone as they are, regardless of their needs. It should go without saying that continued bad behaviours should not go unattended. Don't think you need to accept everything a person does. Learn to recognise the difference between when someone is in need and when they are using a control drama to hold your love.

You need to stand up and search for it within you; wake up and practice it in your life every single day. Make the decision to love unconditionally. From my personal experience, I can tell you that you will love life once you discover the power of unconditional love.

Chapter 10.

DO EVERYTHING WITH LOVE

"Be on guard. Stand firm in the faith. Be men of courage. Be strong. Do everything in love."
– 1 Corinthian 16:13, 14

When I first read this verse in the Bible, I couldn't understand what "do everything in love" meant. The second time around, I had a better idea what it meant, at least intellectually, but I still couldn't feel any love in what I was doing.

Years later, after I discovered my passions and the meaning of life, everything changed for me and I started to do everything with love. The reason that I chose to write this chapter is to inspire you to do everything with love, even the most insignificant things in your life.

There will always be times when we have to do things we don't like, still we do them anyway and learn from them. I don't want to speak with you about your passions in this session. I want to guide you to

149

understanding more about the way you behave and why, the way you do things, think, and act.

The intention behind everything you do is really important and the feeling you put into what you do is more important than the result itself. It may surprise you to learn that your intention and the passion you put into something, whether positively or negatively, will affect the outcome and determine its power. The more passionate you are about doing anything, the more powerful the outcome.

Here's an example of how passion can determine the power of an event.

Suppose you're arguing with your spouse over something small. She becomes annoyed and argues her point to defend her position. You put her down and tell her she's wrong. Now she becomes madder and begins to raise her voice. The passion is building. You want to be right or believe you're right, so you raise your voice in response. Your voice is louder than hers and she begins to cry. Now you're both arguing with high passion. The event has gained power and escalated to the point where it will be memorable. Both parties are hurt and you will have to undo this event with a loving event of equal passion so your mind doesn't latch onto that negative argument.

Believe it or not, you could have had that same argument in a loving way. You could have approached your spouse by simply stating your case without being judgemental of whatever it was you thought she did. If she responded negatively, you would simply refuse to get into a heated argument and try to see her point of view. Why did she do this thing? What motivated her? Is it really important to her? Is it really important to you? Talk about these things as though you were talking to a four year old child, with love. You wouldn't expect a four year old to know what you're thinking or how you feel about a situation. You would have to explain it to them in simple terms. Show that same love to the adults in your life, particularly those you love.

It may be more difficult to do everything with love to everyone, co-workers, strangers, clerks, and so on, but doing so will result in peace with yourself and your world. For some, it may be easier to see love in strangers than in your loved ones because loved ones know how to push your buttons. But be determined to stay happy and determined to express love daily in every single action of your life. I know it's hard, but there is a big reward. You will change for better and your life will become a big adventure as a lover of this life.

I know you do a lot of things in your life, but be honest. How many of these things really matter? How many hold great importance? How many of these things make you happy? How many of these things make you feel alive? Full of life? Love? Hope? What are you really in love with?

You need faith to be able to enjoy and love what you do, you need courage, you need to be on guard, because most of the people on this planet are doing things they don't like, things they don't love and they are not happy at all, so they will affect your dealings with them. What is the point then of doing anything if you're not happy doing it?

Are you the kind of person who wants things to work for you but you don't want to feel any pain or make any effort? Or are you the person that wants to change for better and is willing to look for different ways to improve, to be happy, to love life and to feel fulfilled? Or even better, are you that kind of person who already lives the life you were dreaming of? You worked hard to get here, you were able to pay the price for this fantastic life that now is helping you to inspire others to change their life for better.

Where are you my friend?

Be honest with yourself!

Don't give up. Whatever your position now, you always have the option to change, to create, to make things happen because you are brilliant, full of potential, talents and love; just allow yourself more space, time and dedication to live all of the amazing gifts that you possess.

My goal is to inspire you to develop this mentality of doing everything with love that will completely change your life. This is the most difficult part because most of us have not grown up with this attitude. We grew up with different cultures and mentalities for years and years, so you will need to break the cycle. It will take you a bit of time, but it is worth doing.

I want to help you to see love in everything you do, in every person that you meet, in anything that you achieve, even in the little daily routines, because if you can manage the little things in life you will be able to master the big ones. It's about personal discipline, so you need to train yourself for that.

How do you do it?

Simple. Start every day, from the time you wake up, to put love in everything. That means to be in the present, to care, to pay attention how you brush your teeth, how you make your coffee, the way you speak with your lovers, be gentle, calm, positive, no matter what. Choose to live your day as you want. That means being in charge of your happiness. But let's be honest, how many people are doing that? A few, maybe. Are you one of them or are you the opposite? You can always choose where to be, what to do, and how you want to feel instead of allowing what happens **to** you to control you and how you feel. Doing this will increase your awareness of everything around you and you can choose to make others miserable or use love to edify them.

It is not about ignoring what happens in your life, it's about choosing how to feel and act no matter what life throws at you.

It took me more than 25 years to develop a kind of philosophy of life. I couldn't understand why I should do everything with love, I couldn't see so deep until I tried it in my daily life.

The most important things about love are the things I learnt in the moments that I was suffering, during my dark depression, and during the most challenging situations. I paid the price to understand the power of love and the best way to learn about it is when you don't have it. Doing everything with a love mentality will completely change you as a person and will bring more happiness and fulfilment in your life. Give love before you expect to receive it, be the person that you want to see next to you, be the first one who smiles, who shakes the hand, who helps, supports, encourages, inspires others, be the person you want to see in the world and then you will see the power of this change, you will start to lead and inspire people by your example.

Love is magical, love can hurt you or treat you like a king or queen. Love is the essence of life, it is the ingredient that makes our life so beautiful. When you wake up in the morning and can say **I love my life, I can see love everywhere in my life**, then you understand the power of love and you are living it. There are no words to explain what it means to discover true love, real love, love that can heal you from your past, solve your problems and whatever is in your life that is stopping you from being the person you want to be. Love can be the solution to almost anything. If you've been seeking love, start to love yourself first because love is within you, you have the key, use it for your happiness and fulfilment in this life.

Because there are few in this life who are willing to face the reality of life and learn from it, if you know someone like that, stay close to them, read them, live them, spend time with them, choose to be inspired by them. I wanted to inspire you with my personal story and my personal journey and how I discovered what real unconditional love is.

The next chapter will be the last of this part of the book and one of the most important; we will speak about different ways to express love.

Are you ready? See you on the next page.

Chapter 11.

DIFFERENT WAYS
TO EXPRESS LOVE

"Love is friendship that has caught fire. It is quiet understanding, mutual confidence, sharing and forgiving. It is loyalty through good and bad times. It settles for less than perfection and makes allowances for human weaknesses."
– Ann Landers

What exactly does love mean for you?

How do you describe love with your own words?

Love is not a feeling like most of us believe, but is actually an action that begins in the brain, not the heart.

Actions, emotions, and feelings are different things. Our actions are determined by our emotions and our attitude and our emotions and attitude by our thoughts. How you think is really important to your well-being.

The majority of people on this planet assume that love is between a man and woman, and sometimes family, but there is much more to love. I like to believe that love is like a ghost, a lot of people speak about it and look for it, but just a few have seen it. A lot of people say "I LOVE YOU" but just a few really feel it, understand it, experience it and practice it. But just because you can't see the ghosts around you, it doesn't mean that they don't exist. It's the same with love; if you are not aware enough to feel it or see it in your life, it doesn't mean that it's not within you and around you.

The reason I created this chapter about different ways to express love was because of my personal experience of it and what I learnt and understood from the people around me, how they deal with it and what most people understand about it. I wanted to make clear for you that love has many ways of showing itself between people.

I used to think that love makes us suffer, lose time and energy and breaks our hearts, but that is not true; love itself can't do this; it's always our perception and understanding about it that makes us feel this way.

All our life we are focused on one or two ways that love can be expressed and we think we know all about it. But love has nothing to do with physical attraction, sex, or anything else; love is pure and it's not easy to understand it. You can't discover love when you feel good, only during the bad times. It's like appreciating the top of a high mountain you've climbed. To understand and feel the sensation there on top you need to cross the deepest valley and make the climb. You can't find LOVE living your life in the past or in the future; you need to be aware of the importance of living in the present.

When I first started to understand something about love, I was around ten years old. I had an alcoholic dad and a problematic mum in my family and a younger sister. Most of the time, I had no particular feeling or emotion about love; my parents were usually fighting, punching us and treating us sometimes like animals. We would go for days without food, not a sandwich for school and no dinner before going to bed. And that wasn't all. A few times a week they would send us on the streets to ask for cigarettes for them and collect what people were throwing away... I was a child, but I knew that what they did for me wasn't love. Now I understand that for them, that was their way of expressing their feelings. That was my reality at the time. I couldn't force them to love us in the way I wanted. But too many people do try to control how love is expressed and don't give others the freedom they deserve to express love in their own way.

I still think often about that tough period of my life that made me the person that I am today and I realise that I didn't feel love for them during that period. What I felt was pure attachment and the fear of losing them and being alone. Anyway, in the end, my fear become my reality because they just abandoned us and, from that moment, another important story of my life began.

I shared this piece of my personal story regarding love to make you see that you may never understand love when you are happy. I'm not saying that you need to be sad, but you will discover more about the joy love can bring by living your life with both the big and small waves.

I would like now to share with you different ways to express love and to help you to discover more about it.

Love for humanity

This is the type of love I've been talking about throughout this section of the book. It's the type of love we feel for all humanity and is called **agape love**. It accepts people the way they are beneath the surface. It's the love that we generally have to work on because, although we may not particularly like someone, we can choose to love them knowing they are human, with all the human frailties we ourselves are subjected to.

Passionate love

This is the type of love we express to our partner (wife, girlfriend, boyfriend, or husband). The type of love you show for a partner is **romantic** or **eros love**. It's easy to show love when things are going well in the relationship, but the secret to maintaining a healthy relationship with your partner is to be able to show your love even when things are not going well. You can express it with physical touch and affection, words of affirmation, compliments, gifts, action service, or some other kind of support. This is the kind of love that stirs the soul as well as the loins.

Love for friends and family

I want to speak with you about love for your family and friends as well. This kind of love is called **storge love** and is the type of love that parents show children. It often involves sacrifice and hard commitment. How many times have you felt that your friends were a part of the family? You need to look at them that way, and you will become even closer to your real friends.

Ask yourself how many times you did something for someone not because you had to but because you just wanted too? You were doing it out of love. How did you feel about it? It's magical isn't it? This is the feeling that I'm talking about. Let me tell you something, it doesn't matter your religion, your nationality, your age, your sexuality, or your culture. Everybody needs to be loved and to have some outlet for their own love; it's so beautiful when we can understand the meaning of loving people and start to live everyday with this purpose.

Affectionate love

This type of love is **platonic love**. It goes a step beyond agape love because affection is generally only shown to people we like. You can make the conscious decision to love people you don't like, but you won't necessarily show them affection. You reserve your affection for those you enjoy spending time with, such as friends and family.

Love languages

I read a book a few years ago about love languages and I didn't know any of them before. I thought I knew how to love, but I was wrong.

I got married five months ago and I was so excited. I felt so good and I felt loved. I thought I was being loving, too, but honestly, I discovered how hard it is to maintain that love without becoming discouraged afterwards, when things became difficult, real, and when we started to really get to know each other and the ways we express love.

Humans have a specific way of expressing love, as do all animals. It's unique to our species and each human is unique. There may be similarities, but no two humans are the same and for that reason it's really important to understand how you express love and the way your significant other expresses love. They may not be the same.

So, I got married and I discovered that I didn't know how to be a great husband. I didn't know the way I wanted to be loved and to love and I started to learn and to discover the miracle of love.

Most people think they know how to express love for their partner in what many of us call romantic love, but few really know what it means to show unconditional love to their partners. Give yourself the opportunity to learn and discover about love, every day, every moment of your life and you will know more about yourself and your partner. We usually expect from others the same love we give, but it can't be like this because

159

we are not the same; we are unique and beautiful in the way we are. Let's speak now about some ways to express your love for your partners.

Words of affirmation

How many times have you wanted someone to tell you something to make you feel good? Or how many times have you wanted to hear the phrase 'I love you'? It is so true that 'everybody needs somebody to love'. It's true, it's real, and other than basic survival, it's the one thing human beings need on this planet.

There are different ways to express love and I want to speak with you now about words of affirmation. We understand that love can be expressed in different languages. That means that people have different ways of showing their love. This is their 'language' of love, it's how they are comfortable expressing themselves, their emotions.

Words are one of the most common love languages, but we need to be careful about what we say because it's easy to say the wrong thing or be misunderstood. Most of the time we say something and we feel or think something else. This is dangerous because in time, your real feelings will come up, and they usually come up in an argument where you will express the feelings you've been harbouring. So for any kind of a relationship, it's important to say what you feel, mean what you say and use your words carefully. Words can be used in the wrong way if you are not completely in touch with your feelings. What you feel, think and say need to be congruent or you will miss the point you're trying to make and the persons around you may take you wrong.

Personally, my love language is using words of affirmation. I like to tell her every day how much I love her and what I feel for her. Sometimes I like to write her a letter or send a text. Naturally, making love is part of our love expression, but mostly I use my words and the biggest thing that I discovered after we got married was that she has an entirely different language to express love; she prefers physical touch more than anything else. When we understood this, we tried to balance words with physical touch to enjoy our married life, even if sometimes it was difficult to find a way. The secret is that we were clever enough to create a way when we couldn't find one.

Think about how you like to feel love from someone. Are you a person who likes to hear several times a day, 'I love you'? Do you generally use words to express your feelings and emotions? If you enjoy and feel secure when someone tells you how much they care about you and if you like to tell your partner every day how much love you feel, than words, whether written or spoken, are your love language.

For a successful relationship with your partner, it's really important to know your personal love language and theirs. Both partners need to express love in their own way and learn the language of the other. In this way, you will both feel fulfilled. Too many divorces happen because the partners don't know what the person next to them wants or how to give them what they want. Most people break up because they want to express love, but in a different way than their partner can receive it. Communication will stop, and when that happens, everything will finish. The connection between them will be turned off.

To have a successful relationship, focus on your words and your vocabulary, how you express yourself and your emotions. Starting today, be really careful about **what you say** to your partner and **how you say it**.

Timing is equally important. **When** you say something can make the difference between being heard or not, between having your partner's attention and working against whatever they're doing at the time. If your partner is deep into some important paperwork, for example, and is trying to keep to a deadline, feel them out first. Ask them if they would like to take a break. If they cannot, wait until later to express your thoughts.

Physical touch

Many people prefer to express love through physical touch and affection. There are many reasons why people choose this love language and it's definitely one of the most powerful ways to express love. Physical touch brings credibility to your words and makes the beloved person feel more secure at the same time.

After I got married, I actually discovered that my wife and I use two different love languages; I felt good when I discovered that her language is physical touch. From that moment I started to pay more attention to make a difference in our relationship, to know the way she communicates her feelings and emotions, whereas before I thought we all express love in the same way. Now, after months, we know each other better than before and we continue to learn new things about each other all the time. It is fantastic how we can grow and learn when we are open and when we really care about what we're doing.

Think about your relationship; ask your partner to do these exercises together with you to discover more about yourself and each other, and you will find out that most of the time a good hug (more than a second) is better than saying "I LOVE YOU" ten times. There are moments when a word is enough to go ahead. All you need to do is to spend more quality time with your partner to discover new ways to express yourself and your emotions. The secret is to focus on him/her, not on yourself. In this way, you can learn more about the power of love.

I always had a big picture about love in my mind, but as we saw above, there are many ways to express it and our job is to find our own way and to live it.

I truly believe that living your life with true love is one of the best philosophies so far. You can think about the world with love and try to do your best to make it a better place, treat animals with love and play with them, care about them. Spread love around you and give love unconditionally; this is the most difficult test that we human beings need to pass.

I can tell you that once you start to practice the miracles of love in your life, you will see how you, your life, and the people around you will change. It's something stronger than you; it's amazing because you will realise how beautiful life is and how many things you missed before just because you didn't know how to love; you didn't open your mind and your heart to see the little things of daily life that really matter.

I started years ago, and now I feel even younger, more secure, more beautiful, more positive and more productive. I feel happier, smarter and I have beautiful relationships; because of that, now I can feel the energy of life, of people around me. I can choose now who I want to have in my life and who not, I'm more selective with my friends and I even respect myself. In a few words, the magic of love will wake you up, open your eyes, mind and heart and you will literally be a new and better person.

When I started to write this book I didn't know why I chose the title **LIVE LOVE DREAM**! I felt it was the write one. And now, every single part of the title is filled with meaning; it's a real inspirational book.

In writing Section Two, I understood why I should choose this: because our world, our society needs more love, needs to understand the power of love, needs to live the beautiful life behind it. This is the reason. I wanted to spread this message around with friends and family, to be kinder and gentler, to treat others with love and to see in others always something good. I know it's not easy, but it's my own philosophy of life and I wanted to inspire you to live it, too.

This part of the book was a special one and if you need to read it again, just do it anytime. Refer to it often. It was a pleasure to share my personal experiences with you and show you a different way to express love and live your life. I love to share and teach, to help and support and for that reason I chose to write about love; it's a really delicate subject. People speak less and less about it, so for that reason, let's inspire others by our example. Let's show each other how to live a loving life and how to discover the power of love, every day in every way.

"Be the example that you want to see in the world one day," Gandhi said. Discover the power of love that is in you.

I want to say thank you because you've been with me until now, and I encourage you to join me in the last session of this book, the third part: **DREAM**, one of the most inspirational of this book.

I will speak about, **DREAMS**, **GOALS**, and **PLANS**; about **YOU**.

See you next chapter my friend.

Enjoy!

PART III

DREAM

Chapter 12.

WHAT DOES IT MEAN TO DREAM?

"Life is full of beauty. Notice it. Notice the bumble bee, the small child and the smiling faces. Smell the rain and feel the wind. Live your life to the fullest potential and fight for your dreams."
– Ashley Smith

What does it mean to dream?

I'm not referring to sleeping dreams, but the kind of dreams we have during our waking hours, the things we envision for ourselves. They used to simply be called daydreams, but with modern exploration into how the mind works, we now know they are thoughts that we would like to manifest into reality.

Your dreams are unique to you. They are in that fabulous and magical part of the mind that allows you to be or do whatever you want! Whatever you dream you can live! Does this sound too beautiful to be true?

Yes, it is true! It's real and it's true!

167

Again, I'm not speaking about your night time dreams; I'm speaking about your life dreams, about your desires, your ambitions, your goals and plans in this life. In one word, I'm speaking about **YOU**!

This is one of my favourite sections of this book because it shows us the possibilities that life can bring us!

I love it!

I love to speak about dreams and goals because I'm a dreamer and an achiever, and for me speaking about it makes me feel super motivated and determined and actually really excited about it.

Do you have any dreams in this life? Any desires? Think about it for a while. How do you feel? What do your dreams look like? Are they actually yours? Can you make them a reality? Do they make you feel scared? Or cry? Or excited? It's really important to understand how you feel when you speak about your dreams and goals. You will see why it's so important to know your emotions and associate them with your dreams.

I'm one of the biggest dreamers on this planet and one of the hungry achievers, so we will have a lot of fun in this last section of this book. I want you to open your heart, your mind and your eyes, to be here with me 100% and to absorb everything you need to make your dreams your reality.

What does it really mean to dream?

We all have dreams and desires in life, but being aware of them and doing something about them helps you to wake up and give meaning to your dreams. I'm speaking about your inner world and what you want to do and who you want to become. So dreaming means that you want something more, you don't want to settle, you desire more, you want to achieve more, to become more, to expand and grow to become a better person.

I remember there was a time in life when all I had were my dreams, my desires, my plans, and my goals, and I discovered that having only dreams at that particular time was enough for me! Why? Because my dreams gave me the power to move forward, to do something, to create something.

I had the biggest dreams when I was ten years old. I had to drop out of school and go to work to bring food home for my family. That experience helped me learn the power of responsibilities, to become a man at an early age, to believe in my dreams and do something about them! I thought about my dreams all the time. I got power and motivation from them to move forward and to create a way to realise my dreams. It wasn't easy at all, but I made it, and that means that it's possible to make your dreams come true, to live them and make them your reality.

I was broken hearted after my parents abandoned me. I was suffering when they left; I felt so much pain and my dreams were the only thing that gave me hope, courage and determination to do something. It gave me the strength to not give up, to fight and to create a vision about what I wanted to do. I didn't know that much at that time. I just wanted to become someone to help people and to create a better world. The biggest dream was to go to school again. I wanted the opportunity to show my potential and study what I liked.

Having dreams and fighting to make them your reality will help you become a stronger person; it will help you to become more confident, more inspired and more powerful. Perhaps most importantly, it will help you create a vision about yourself.

I learnt how to dream when I literally hit rock bottom, when I couldn't see anything positive in that situation. That was more than 12 years ago. Dreaming may even help you heal yourself from the past and one of the most important things about dreaming is that you can create a powerful vision to see things that other people can't see for you!

169

My goal in this session about dreaming is to inspire and motivate you to understand the power and meaning of dreams and to show you how you can live a better life if you fight and follow your dreams.

Now be honest with yourself:

- How much time have you put into making one of your dreams come true?
- How many times have you sacrificed something for one of your dreams?
- How many times have you dedicated yourself to your dreams?
- How many times have you given up on your dreams even before you started to do something about them?

Do you like the answers you've given? How do you feel about this? Can you do better? Of course you can!

You have the opportunity to work on your dreams every single day and the more you work for them the more you discover yourself and how magical you are. You don't need someone else's approval to do that, you just need to start to care more about it and to take action.

The big difference between people is this: most of them don't know anything about themselves and what their dreams are. They ended up working for other people's dreams and guess what? They have never been happy because they felt that something was always missing from their life. Of course it was. It's natural. They are spending all their life doing something for other people who had the courage to fight and follow their dreams and who now are enjoying the rest of their life and dreaming every day for more and better.

Do you know anyone in this situation?

Do you know anyone who has killed their own dreams to work for other people's dreams? Or are you in that situation? This is really a sad thing, to give away your life just because you don't have the courage to fight and do something for what you want and desire in life!

Now ask yourself, **where am I**? Where do **you** fit in with this at the moment? Are you happy with your life and your reality? Or can you do better? You can start today, right now, doing something about it! No more excuses! From now on, start to care about you and about your life. Give yourself a deadline. Start to make a plan to live your dreams.

Stay with me my friend and enjoy this fabulous session about dreams because I have even more beautiful news about it! I discovered that dreaming makes you feel free. It helps you to access freedom and richly experience your life, to see that life is actually beautiful and full of opportunities every single day. Life is a blessing and by doing this you will become aware about you and the beauty of your life.

Let's do one powerful exercise that you may never have done, just to start this session in the best way!

Write your 10 biggest life dreams. If you've never done this before or something similar, it will be a bit difficult for you, but give it a try! You might have more dreams or less, but for now write down just 10. Don't skip this exercise! It's really simple and one of the most important of this book. Let's do it!

1. _____   2. _____

3. _____   4. _____

5. _____   6. _____

7. _____   8. _____

9. _____   10. _____

How do you feel now that you have completed the exercise?

Do you feel different to how you felt minutes ago before the exercise? If so, it's because your dreams are recognised by the brain the same way it recognises an image. For every single image, you experience different emotions and feelings that are associated with it. It's really powerful. You should feel more excited, motivated and positive if you've done the exercise honestly.

One of the biggest fears of most of us is to **not** succeed in life, but you will be successful if you pursue your dreams. By living your life with passion and courage, you commit yourself to doing something that most people don't. We have to live life with dreams all the time. Your dreams make you unique and you will lead by your example; keep looking for your dreams and discover them.

One of the biggest human issues is that we give up too easily when things become hard. Worse, people give up on their dreams even before starting because of the way the human mind works. Thoughts are influenced by our experiences, telling us most of the time that we **can't** do this and that or we are **not good enough**, but let me tell you that you are a star and you can achieve anything you want if you have a big **why** to motivate you.

There was a time in my life when I had a lot of dreams. I felt so lucky because I knew one day I would achieve them; I believed so much, with all my heart, that everything I wanted would happen. You need to believe, you need to train yourself to be open minded and learn more, become more and dream even more. I can write a book just about dreaming; it's one of my favourite topics.

I want you now to think about your biggest dream in this life, apart from the 10 you've already listed above. I do usually ask people when I meet them, "What's your biggest dream?" And most of them, actually around

172

90%, don't know how or what they need to answer me and this makes me feel so sad. From their answers I can understand if that person has a good vision and life purpose or they just live day by day with no real direction.

Many of the people that I ask tell me, "I don't know, I never thought about it." And this is the first thing you should think about it. The more you learn how to dream, the more a vision for your life will come to you; you will get a sense of the direction you should be taking, a sense of meaning and you will know what to do, when and how.

A few people respond to me later about what they want to do or what they want to achieve and because you are reading this book, I suppose I can say we've met already. So I will take the permission to ask you: **WHAT'S YOUR BIGGEST DREAM?** What's your biggest WHY? By answering these questions, you will get power and you will become more aware about your potential.

I don't know what your dreams are, but let me tell you that it's possible to make them happen. It may not be easy, there may be a lot of pain and sacrifice and you will need to push yourself over and over to get the life that you want.

The number one rule in life is:

Don't give up on your dreams!!!

This is a rule for people who want to make a difference in their life and inspire others to do the same. ☺ You need to believe that you can do it!

Don't live a life that you are not happy with, don't let the fear of failure influence you. Overcome it by thinking about and envisioning the outcome you desire or what your life will be like if you don't do it. Start to learn how to work on yourself and your dreams. You don't want to live the life of other people; you want to live your dream life. Now it's possible if you start to invest in you and change your attitude, to believe in yourself and not give up no matter how difficult it gets. Continually tell yourself that you are going to just do it! A lot of other people did it and I'm sure you can do it, too. I'm proof that it's possible. I literally started with nothing, on the streets, with no parental help or guidance and with virtually no money. You need a big WHY in order to follow your dreams, to fight for them and make the reality that you desire. It's really important that you understand and **believe** that you can live your dreams. A person that lives their life without living their dreams is like a zombie, moving in a half dead state with no hope for a better future.

What about you? Are you brilliant? A star?

Or do you just survive, going through life like a zombie, unhappy and frustrated? Let me tell you that it can be difficult and take time to get to the point where you can live the life you want, but it's worth the effort. Give to that life as much as you can, do your best and be YOU! Live that freedom. Free yourself from your own prison called 'negative mind'. Stop repeating thoughts like: **I can't, I'm nobody, I'm not enough, I'm too young, too old** and **I have no skills!** Step up and pursue your dreams, share them and do something to make them reality. Remember, the mind replays your thoughts over and over again and those thoughts become your reality. So why not make them positive thoughts about what you want from life? It's just as easy to make those positive thoughts become your reality as it was to make negative thoughts manifest.

I want to share with you a few strategies that you can use every day to help you pursue your dreams. You are rich in dreams! Even if you are a millionaire now, that money is merely a tool to make your life easier, but it won't necessarily make you feel fulfilled. But your dreams are yours; they are a unique part of you, and for that reason I want to share with you what I learnt when I started to become a dreamer and later an achiever.

There is nothing quite as empowering as the moment you realise you have reached your dreams. Sometimes we can allow excuses and self-limiting beliefs to prevent us from setting our dreams and goals as high as we truly desire in our hearts. There are hundreds of things we can tell ourselves about why we will never actually achieve what it is we are yearning for. It could be we feel we don't have the time, money, strength or support. Perhaps we believe we aren't smart enough, talented enough or deserving enough to have what we dream about, or we believe that it's an impossible undertaking. When we live life believing we can't reach our goals, we will prove ourselves right every time. Not only will we lose that sense of accomplishment, over time we may stop dreaming altogether. We are all deserving of success and happiness. We owe it to ourselves to aim high in life and to go after what we truly want. We are meant to live fully and experience what life has to offer.

On the journey to pursue your goals and dreams, you have the opportunity to learn valuable life lessons that will help you see that anything is possible. Are you ready for the strategies?

Let's go!

These are the 7 most powerful strategies to transform your dreams and goals into reality and get what you want.

Strategy 1: Dream it.

This is crucial. Everything begins in the heart and mind. Every great achievement began in the mind of one person. They dared to dream, to believe that it was possible. Take some time to allow yourself to ask, "What if?" Think big. Don't let negative thinking discourage you. You **want** to be a dreamer. Dream of all the possibilities for yourself, your family and for others. If you had a dream that you let grow cold, re-ignite the dream! Fan the flames. Life is too short to let it go. Live your life on your own terms.

Strategy 2: Believe it.

Yes, your dream needs to be big. It needs to be something that is seemingly beyond your capabilities. But it also must be believable. You must be able to say that if certain things take place, if others help, if you work hard enough, though it is a big dream, it can still be done. Here is a good example: A person with no college education can dream that he will build a $50 million-a-year company. That is big, but believable. Bad example: A 90-year-old woman with severe arthritis in her hips, knees, and ankles who hasn't exercised in 25 years will run a marathon in under three hours. It is big all right, but not very likely. She might stand a better chance of building a $50 million-a-year business! And she better get a move on! Now write down your own real example. Continue to believe!

Strategy 3: Visualise it!

The great achievers have a habit. They "see" things. They picture themselves walking around their CEO office in their new $25 million corporate headquarters, even while they are sitting on a folding chair in their garage "headquarters." Great free-throw shooters in the NBA picture the ball going through the basket. PGA golfers picture the ball going straight down the fairway. World-class speakers picture themselves speaking with energy and emotion. All of this grooms the mind to control the body to carry out the dream. What can you see right now? What pictures do you play in your mind?

Strategy 4: Share it.

One reason many dreams never go anywhere is because the dreamer keeps it all to himself. It is a quiet dream that only lives inside his mind. The one who wants to achieve their dream must tell that dream to many people. Why? As we continually say it, we begin to believe it more and more. If we are talking about it then it must be possible. Furthermore, it holds us accountable. When we have told others, it spurs us on to actually doing it so we don't look foolish.

Strategy 5: Plan it.

Every dream must take the form of a plan. The old saying that you "get what you plan for" is so true. Your dream won't just happen. You need to take time out on a regular basis to plan your strategy for achieving the dream. Think through all of the details. Break the whole plan down into small workable parts. Then set a time frame for accomplishing each task on your "dream plan". Do it every day. It's magical.

Strategy 6: Work it.

Hey, wouldn't life be grand if we could quit before this one! Unfortunately, the successful are usually the hardest workers. While the rest of the world is sitting on their sofas watching TV, achievers are working on their goal—achieving their dream. I have an equation that I work with: Your short-term tasks multiplied by time equal your long-term accomplishments. If you work on it each day, eventually you will achieve your dream. Leo Tolstoy wrote *War and Peace*, more than 1200 pages, in longhand, page by page. Why can't you do it? Push yourself to do it and it will happen.

Strategy 7: Enjoy it.

That's the part that I love! When you have reached your goal and you are living your dream, be sure to enjoy it. In fact, enjoy the trip, too. Give yourself some rewards along the way. Give yourself a huge reward when you get there. Help others enjoy it. Be gracious and generous. Use your dream to better others. Then go back to Strategy 1. And dream a little bigger this time! You can do it!

Now you have powerful strategies to practice every single day to achieve your dreams and goals. Start as soon as possible using them on your personal journey.

177

This was the first session of this amazing and last part of the book about dreams and goals. Remember, you can become better and better if you want to! You need to focus and one of the most important things is to be self-disciplined if you want to achieve great things.

I will speak to you in the next session!

Continue to believe and live your life with passion! Fight for your **DREAMS**!

Chapter 13.

WHY DO WE HAVE DREAMS?

"Love what you do and do what you love. Don't listen to anyone else who tells you not to do it. You do what you want, what you love. Imagination should be the centre of your life. Wish it, Dream it, and Make it Happen."
Ray Bradbury

I do believe that this life doesn't have any meaning without dreaming. We have dreams and because they are the centre of our life, whatever you realised until now in your life is because you first dreamt it, imagined it, you visualised something before it became a reality. Actually, we dream every day and night, but there is a big difference between night dreams and waking dreams. We dream because it's the way our brains and minds are wired. Night dreams are created by the psyche. They help solve or sort out problems. And if you're astute at deciphering their meaning, they can help you see things from a different perspective. Waking dreams

179

are created by the imagination. When you imagine something, you can make it happen.

> *"All men dream, but not equally. Those who dream by*
> *night in the dusty recesses of their minds wake in the day*
> *to find that all was vanity. But the dreamers of the day are*
> *dangerous men, for they may act their dream with open eyes*
> *and make it possible."*
> – T. E. Lawrence

All dreams matter, but it's up to you to decide which ones you want to pursue and which you do not; whatever you choose will affect your future life. It's good to start to become more aware about your dreams. The dreams you focus on and are more aware of will be the ones that shape your destiny here on this planet. Live with purpose, work hard and convert your dreams into reality. You can see the beauty of life through your imagination, your vision, and your dreams and you will become more aware of your situation and opportunities available to you. Live your life, live your dreams and become the person that you're meant to be. Wish it, dream it and make it happen.

I started to dream of a better life from the age of eight, but my dreams were not clear. Then from age ten, they started to become clearer. This was actually a real dream where I had more needs and desires for a better life. I remember very well when I was going to school without food and I had to ask for something to eat. In that moment, my dream was to have a family that can provide me with food and support and by the time I grew up, still without family, a place to call my own, or a real income, I understood that I needed to accept that reality because I wasn't able in that moment to change it!

I saw my colleagues going on amazing school trips and I wanted to go, but I couldn't. I saw them with parents and being supported whereas I wasn't. I saw them with new clothes and shoes, which I hadn't. And all the time in my mind I repeated to myself, **"One day I will have food, clothes, trips and a happy family."** And what happened is so powerful! In my mind I started to create pictures about it and I told myself that I would find the way to have all those things that I didn't have and if I did not find the way, I would create one. I didn't know how, but I knew **why**, and that was enough.

I remember one of the strongest desires I had in my mind after my parents abandoned us was to have a happy family. This picture of a happy family was something I always had in my mind and guess what? It happened before the deadline I had set for myself. With persistence and believing that it was going to happen, my mind converted a strong desire into a real dream. It caused me to actually go in that direction. (And this is why negative self-talk will work for you in the **wrong** direction).

The beautiful thing is that after a few years and a few serious relationships, one with an amazing human being, Lena (my first love), I met Alina, a magical girl from the church I used to go to. One of the reasons I fell in love with her was her beautiful voice when we sang worship songs in the church. When I moved from the city, after a while I met Elena, one of the strongest women that I've been with, beautiful and sensitive, one of my first loves. I moved to Bucharest for University and when I'd been to Germany to do volunteering, I met Rachele, an Italian woman, with blond hair and green eyes. I remember very well that I told myself, "She is the ONE". With her I had one of the longest and most beautiful relationships ever. She actually taught me a lot and with her I discovered another world.

I am honest and I can tell that every single woman that I've been with taught me a lot and I am grateful because they helped me to become a man and to discover myself. Each one of these women taught me to dream in a different way. I was so lucky to meet fabulous women like them and I'm still in contact with all of them. I'm amazed to see how everyone grew in different ways. Not all relationships last, but whether you're currently single or married, say thank you to all the women (or men) who taught you to dream along the way. Each one helped you in your life.

From the age of 14, I had a few relationships and when I was about 24, I took a break for two years to discover myself and learn what I wanted from life. I needed to figure out how I was going to get what I wanted and set a potential deadline for achieving that.

I don't know where you are in your life or what your current situation is, but let me tell you that where you are now is the result of your past dreams, desires, visions and whatever you have been paying the most attention to. If you are happy and everything is okay in your life, that's great for you. If not, then you can only take responsibility for your lack of dreams, plans and visions about what you want.

Now that you know how thoughts become reality, if you have a dream and you want to make it happen, you first need to believe that it's possible; that's the number one rule! Remember, belief lives in the mind. Nothing is going to change if you don't believe that life itself is a magical thing and that you can make things change!

I use to live in Rome, Italy where I finished one of my master's degrees to become a trainer, speaker and coach. Later, I lived in Naples for more than 2 years and this is where I started to work as a coach for students. I organised some seminars and courses about personal development. Everything was okay materially, but deep down I was looking for more, for better. I wanted to grow, I wanted to discover more about life and about myself, so I had a conversation with some close friends. One of them was Pasquale, Rachele's father.

After talking to Pasquale, I made the decision to move to London, England. This was a risk, but I bought just a one way ticket. I didn't want to come back. I moved there with plans and goals and I was willing to pay whatever the price was for my dreams.

My friend, if you really want to change your life, you need to make a big decision. Don't be afraid of the outcome; take the leap and be responsible for the way your life turns out. It's very empowering.

I moved to London in the beginning of July, 2014, just after my birthday. ☺ My English wasn't good at all and most of the time I used to say "yes" and "no" to whatever people around me were saying.

It was hard in the beginning. I was living in a hostel and had just breakfast each day. I walked every day more than 10 km trying to find a job, whatever job, just something to make money. I remember feeling very alone, no friends, no family, and no support. Every day I counted my money. All the money I had was £400, and that included money I borrowed from Rachele's family. Within two weeks, my money was gone and I had to leave the hostel. I didn't know what to do. I started crying and I thought about giving up, going back to Italy where I at least knew someone and I had something to do. I remember I felt horrible. I couldn't see any solution for a few days. I was waiting for someone to call me to tell me that I was hired, but I knew this wasn't really going to happen because I was living in an English speaking country and my English wasn't good. I didn't know where to go and ask for help.

The last day of my stay at the hostel I woke up and I told myself that I didn't want to go back. Even if I did want to, I couldn't because I had no money for the ticket. I repeated to myself that I would find a way. I contacted Max Formisano, one of my mentors and a friend, and I explained to him what I was doing and where I was and he was happy for me that I made the decision to get out of my comfort zone and push myself to grow and achieve great things in life. I told Max I needed help, I needed some money and he asked me how much I wanted. I told him I needed enough for one more week in the hostel! He actually sent me money straight away that same day and I paid the hostel for another week.

I learnt a big lesson at that time. For the first time in my life, I learnt how to ask for help. I had never done that before. I had always tried to do everything on my own, but I realised it wasn't so bad to ask for help from someone that knows me and cares about me, even if he was a mentor. I could/should have learned this lesson when my sister and I were begging for food from our neighbours, but at the time, I was more ashamed than anything else, so I pushed it out of my mind. Now, an older young man, I was using reason as my guide. I knew that I would need to sacrifice my pride to have a chance to stay in London.

After a week, nothing happened. The money was gone again and this time I didn't have any other opportunities to ask for money because I didn't know too many people. My sister Catalina wasn't in a position at that moment to help me. I had to leave the hostel. So, with tears in my eyes and pain in my heart I did it! I didn't know where I should go and this time I had nothing to fall back on. I told myself that if I can't find a way to go forward, I will create one. The reason I pushed that much is that I believed in myself. I believed I could do it.

I filled out more than 50 applications. I was already on the street with my bag, some books, my PC and a lot of thoughts and worries. I felt scared about my unknown future.

Then I remembered a big place I had seen when first I moved to London – Victoria tube Station. I decided to go there and I arrived around 10 pm. There were still a lot of people around. I felt hungry, but I didn't have any food, so to forget about it. I started to read my book until I fell asleep. I woke up around 4 am and saw people all around me, people just like me, sleeping on the floor and, for the first time in London, I felt I had friends. For almost a week that station became my home. I will never forget it!

Remember my friend that if you have a big **WHY** in your life, you will find the **HOW**! The more obstacles you come across in your life, the stronger you become and no one will keep you from achieving your dreams. We have dreams to make this world a better place, to become better people and to enjoy the beauty of life.

After almost a week sleeping on the floor in Victoria tube Station, one day I received a call from a man.

"Hi there, is this Ionut?"

I said, "Yes."

"I would like to invite you for an interview." His name is Andrew. My first manager in London who later became my friend. He is an amazing human being. I will be forever grateful for his help and guidance. He offered me a job, without speaking English well and having no experience at all.

The next second I started crying like a baby!!! I was so happy and excited even though I didn't know what the job interview was about. Finally, I felt that someone heard my prayers. And everything started from there. The story is long and fantastic, ☺ painful and inspirational and you can hear it all if you join one of my events or seminars. But I don't want to leave you hanging, so I will tell you more about it.

After three years in London, you may not believe it, after working hard on myself, and on my dreams to create my future, I got married to one of the most beautiful women on this planet, Mina! She stole my heart and I fell in love with her, but that's another beautiful and powerful story of my life. Now, we have a little and special angel Isaia. Our baby taught us so many things and we are open to learn a lot on this journey. Even if between us it didn't work, in the end, our love brought to the world a special soul Isaia who we incredibly grateful for. We managed to stay in touch, to be friends, to respect and support each other and possibly to be the best parents in this world.

All the magical things in my life started to happen when I started to open my mind and myself to the world and to choose to give and share love with others. Now people come to my events every month and I can see them growing and becoming better people. I am so happy and fulfilled, but I'm still dreaming big and setting goals every single day. I actually became obsessed about doing my best every single day; I want to enjoy life and make the best of every minute of my life. I realised that life is so precious, is so beautiful, so wild, so painful and so valuable that I couldn't afford to miss it! You need to live life on your terms; you are in charge. Don't wait for the right moment, create it now! Whatever you want to do, do it now because the 'right moment' will never come. The right moment is NOW.

I'm so happy and grateful that I have had this opportunity to write this book and to share with you my personal story about how I overcame all my life obstacles. Nothing was stopping me from achieving my goals and dreams and I can tell you that I'm just in the beginning of my journey here. I'm a student of life and I want to be the best!

In this session I have explained why we have dreams and how important they are in our life. You will become a powerful person if you fight and follow your dreams. It's going to be somewhat difficult, but you can do it! Every time you come across an obstacle, just remember why you're doing it and imagine the vision that you created in your mind about yourself and your future. I believe everything in this life happens for a reason, so don't focus on what happened. Focus on what you want to see happen next, how you can do better, become better, be brilliant and shine. This is the reason why we have dreams and why we are here.

Without dreams, life has no meaning. We are nothing; we are without purpose. We have no direction and therefore have created nothing to live for, to look forward to. Think about your life. You started to dream when you were little and most of the time people around you said you can't/ shouldn't dream that much because life is hard and the reality is different than your dreams. Now I really want to ask you: **how many times have you written your dreams on a piece of paper? And how many times have you planned something to achieve? How many times have you set a goal, even a short term one?** Be honest with yourself. You see my friend, that's the reason why most of us complain and blame others for our situation. We are not focused on our dreams, but on other people's dreams, and then we become jealous because they achieve things and we don't. You need to train your mind to see the beauty of life and to use your full potential to achieve your dreams.

One of the biggest mistakes that most of us make is to compare ourselves with other people, compare our dreams with theirs, compare our family and house and money with others' and actually compare our happiness with their happiness. Each of us has a meaning and a unique journey. Don't measure yourself against anyone else. Look at your progress and determine how to do better to achieve your dreams. When you stop comparing yourself with others, you will start living and enjoying your life. If you don't, you will always be frustrated and unhappy.

We all have different dreams. This is part of what makes us different and unique. Most of the time, we achieve goals and dreams that are not ours because we try to copy or be like someone else and here is the starting point of the pain. You will not feel fulfilled living someone else's dream, working for someone else's vision, and collecting a pay check doing someone else's work. This is one of the biggest lessons I learnt since I started this amazing journey into personal growth. If you start to apply what I'm sharing with you in this book, you will transform your life forever as I did on myself and remember to practice, practice, and practice until you get it! Don't give up! It's too easy to give up. Stay in the game, be proud to be alive and do your best every day.

Chapter 14.

DREAMING MAKES YOU UNIQUE & UNSTOPPABLE

"No matter where you're from, your dreams are valid."
– L. Nyong'o

I lived for about a year in Naples, Italy. I was doing very well there, but one day I felt I wanted to change something. Do you know this feeling? I think so. I asked myself, "Where can I go to grow in the way I want? Where is there a place in the world that now offers me all the opportunity to realise my dreams?" For months I researched on the internet and I found out that London was the place. Now I've been living in London since July, 2014, and the decision to move there has changed my life for the better every day. I chose to follow my heart and intuition, I chose to fight and take a risk for my dreams, and the hard work has paid off. It opened many doors and gave me the opportunity to express myself and to develop my potential and skills and by doing this I discovered how powerful I can be.

189

We become powerful when we have dreams and goals and plans to strive for, when we have something to live for, something meaningful and beautiful. I found out that every person who has done something to make their dreams a reality, actually finds their uniqueness. In the end, it's our dreams that make us unique.

If you've had moments in your life when you felt so bad, hurt and hit from all that happened in your life and you lost the courage and determination to move forward, if you can't find the power to stand up again, my friend, I'm here with you, I can understand you and I'm here to support you. Every time you feel down, the best thing to do is to accept that you feel like that, to understand that the best you can do is actually to create a way to become stronger than before. But there is something that I want to share with you, my friend. The best exercise is to think about your dreams and goals and imagine achieving them. It will help to motivate you every time you feel you can't do it!

This year (2017) I'm training for the Virgin London Marathon. I have to wake up at 5 am and go to the gym. In the beginning, it was really hard for me, but I always try to imagine myself at the finish line and I push myself to go to the gym. You need self-discipline if you want to make your dreams a reality. You need to self-educate and master your mind to make things happen when everything becomes harder. You need self-discipline for whatever you want to do in your life.

You will discover how unique and powerful you are when you understand the meaning of dreaming. We all have the ability and skills to achieve our dreams and goals. We just need to unlock this inner potential within us, but to do this we need to focus on our personal growth and learn how to access this power.

What do you think **D.R.E.A.M** means? Or what does it mean for you? I started to write it down and I discovered what we need to make our dreams reality. I'm really happy and excited to share this with you!

(D) – DETERMINATION

Are you a determined person? You may have good talents, skills and experience, but if you don't have determination you will never accomplish anything big in your life. Determination is a personal characteristic that will support you when the way becomes hard and when you face difficult moments that threaten to throw you off your course.

(R) – RESPONSIBILITY

This is one of the most powerful characteristics you can develop. When I was a child, my parents were not responsible when it came to their lives or the lives of their children. Ironically, I learnt from them how to be responsible for everything in my life. You learn how to become responsible by owning your actions, words and commitments. When you make a mistake, allow it. You've made your decisions and your mistakes are your own. You are responsible for them. In the same way, when your plans work well for you, you can claim the responsibility for that, too. You can be proud that you did this.

(E) – EDUCATION

Most of us go through the normal process of studying and finishing school. After that, we're no longer interested in studies or learning something new to grow and make an impact in the world and in our personal life, partly because we're not taught that learning is essential for our growth and partly because we've become disillusioned by the school system. But realise that we are here in a continuous process of learning because life itself is like a school; if you want to be a student of life and learn how to enjoy this journey, focus on the process and don't attach yourself to things that don't have any meaning for you.

I remember being an orphan and not having money to pay for my studies, so it seemed as though I couldn't achieve my dreams. My financial situation was grim. Then I asked myself what I might do to make this happen. I started to think of different ways to make money

191

to pay for my studies and to be able to do what I love to do. I got two part-time jobs. I was **determined** to get that diploma, learn new skills, gain knowledge and improve the quality of my life. I was taking **responsibility** for getting an **education**.

My advice to you, my friend, is to look at your goals and dreams and focus on them. Do not focus on what stops you from achieving them. Change your focus and you will change your mind, choose to study and invest in yourself. It's the worthiest investment that you can ever make.

(A) – ACTION

Taking action requires self-discipline, commitment and responsibility. Are you a person that takes action? Are you a person that always takes the initiative? Are you an active or passive person? Do you act? Or react? You need to know yourself before you challenge yourself in any big adventure.

The difference between who you are and who you want to become is actually the action that you take (or don't take). You have the power; no one can do it for you. How many times have you wanted to do something and you had it in your mind then forgot about it? You changed it, you abandoned it or cancelled it? Most of us are stuck and we don't know why. It's actually because of the habit of procrastination and allowing too many distractions to take over. They make us really busy with things that really don't matter or are not important to our growth. These things don't move us forward toward our goal.

When you take action, you become powerful. You make things happen. You become free. If you don't like your job anymore, change it; if you're not happy with your relationship, fix it or change it. If you feel misunderstood by your friends, make a choice to work at the friendship or form new ones. You want to lose weight, jump into the gym. If you want to be happy, train your mind. If you want to grow and be free, find your passion. If you want to enjoy the beauty of this life, find your purpose. If you want to feel fulfilled, TAKE ACTION.

(M) – MOTIVATION

What does **motivation** mean?

Motivation is something that keeps you working towards achieving goals and dreams. It keeps you doing what you have to do to make that thing happen. Motivation is the inner force that is driving you all the time in life; it's the powerful energy inside you that is moving you in the direction of what you want to accomplish.

Are you a motivated person? Or self-motivated?

So many times, we want to do something but we don't feel motivated enough. Isn't that true? Do you recognise the feeling? It's so difficult to be self-motivated to do something. No one is pushing or prodding you to move forward. (This is where having a mentor will help you). You really need a strong reason, you need to know why you have to do that thing. Don't become addicted to someone else to motivate you; learn how to motivate yourself and how to become stronger and more powerful.

Now you know what the word **DREAM** stands for. What will you do next? Can you see and understand the power of this word? The real meaning of the dreams in your life? And how your dreams can make you a unique person? Actually you are unique because we were created as unique souls, but we are responsible for letting our uniqueness shine, for letting it out. Each of us is talented and full of love and beauty in our own way. Yes, including you. I'm speaking about you. When someone lives their dreams they feel full of life, they're happy and they can see the meaning of life in everything. Are you that kind of person? If yes, well done, keep it up. If not, what are you waiting for? What are you doing with your life? What is the biggest dream you want to achieve? Are you dreaming big?

Let me tell you about it in the next chapter. **DO YOUR BEST!** ☺

Chapter 15.

DREAM BIG WITH OPEN EYES

"When you cease to dream, you cease to live."
– Malcolm Forbes

Are you ceasing to live because you've abandoned your dreams?

What are you doing on this planet? Are you committed to paying the price, whatever it takes, to live your dreams?

Or are you one of the millions and billions of people on this planet who go through life without knowing how beautiful it can be when they follow their dream and their heart?

Maybe you're part of the small group of people who dream big, so big that every single one of your dreams scared you enough to push you out of your comfort zone to learn something new, to grow toward those dreams.

I learnt to dream so big that I sometimes thought I dreamt too much. Most of the people I met always told me I was dreaming too big, that I was being unrealistic, but later on I understood that actually they were thinking too small, in accordance with their own reality.

It's so beautiful to be a dreamer. We all have dreams, some have more or less, but when it comes time to sacrifice for them to make them reality, too many people give up. They're not willing or afraid to put in the time and work. And when they do that they start to die little by little from within, until they can't support that pain anymore and they start to self-destruct. This fact makes me feel so bad and it is for that reason I inspire people to fight for their dreams. Your dream is worthy, it's priceless, it's your life, you need to protect it, to defend it; don't allow anyone to tell you that you can't do it, or that it's not for you. Follow your heart and your dreams, find your way and live your life with purpose. You can do it. I did it and others have done it and you can do it, too.

Being a child, around 14 years old, most of the time with nothing in my stomach, I remember that I was always thinking and dreaming that someone somehow would come to give me food and care about be. I remember being at the home protection centre and dreaming of having a house and a happy family, of having the opportunity to study and show my best and I tried to find out how I could make this happen. I wanted to study at one of the best universities in my country, Romania. The best was in the capital, Bucharest. When I told my educators there at the centre that I wanted to study at the University of Bucharest, they started laughing in my face, thinking that I was joking. They said to me, "Who do you think you are? You can't go there to study, you don't have money, you don't know anyone, plus you are from home protection, you definitely don't have any chance to go there to study."

I felt so bad. I understood that they were trying to tell me that they couldn't even go there and I couldn't either. I saw in their eyes they were disappointed with themselves and they weren't happy at all. I went back into my little room and I started crying. I felt that they didn't understand me. They actually couldn't see what I saw at that moment; they didn't have the vision I had because they didn't dream anymore. They gave up on everything apart from their job to survive. Not all of the educators were like this, but most of them. They couldn't motivate me and inspire me because they didn't even do that for themselves.

Even though they told me it wasn't possible, I told myself that I would find a way to go there to study because it was my DREAM!!! I asked them what possibility I had to go there with their support and the answer was, "We can't support you there in any way. It's too far and we can't cover your expenses there. Sorry."

That answer I will never forget! I started to believe even more that I could go and study there. I could feel it, see it, even if they were thinking too small. I asked again, for the third time, and this time they told me if I wanted to go, I would need to write a letter. They told me I would have to do it on my own, but I would not be able to be part of this home protection program. If I left, I would be on my own.

I felt good and bad at the same time. It was a very strange feeling. I felt ice (fear) and fire (determination) inside me at the same time. I quickly told them that I wanted to write the letter and go as soon as possible. I spent a full summer studying with my sister who helped me a lot. I chose to take the train for the first time to Bucharest, to take the most important exam in my life up to that time. I had so many sensations and too many feelings. The one thing I was sure of was that I wanted to pass the exam to officially become a student at the University of Bucharest.

After two days, the results of the exam came. I was so excited, I started to cry and I felt like the happiest person in the world! One of my biggest dreams just became reality. I was officially IN! In some way my life literally started to change from that moment. I had to provide everything for myself; I needed a job plus time to go to the courses. I promised myself that I would be willing and able to pay any price. I felt so good. I had proven to others that they were wrong about me and my dream. Honestly, I felt so much satisfaction. Living my real life started from here. I got two jobs, part-time, one during the night and one during the day, plus I went to seminars, classes and made time to study. For more than two years I was so busy with study and work that I couldn't do anything else, apart from going to the church on Sundays to pray for all and to say how grateful I was for being there and having those opportunities. I promised myself – I didn't know how – that I would become the best!

The second year, after the exams session, they announced that a really big European scholarship program was coming, Erasmus. I didn't know what it was about, but I wanted to try a new experience and to learn something new. This exchange program wasn't for all the students, just for the best ones and on selected numbers, not all of them, just a few in every country. Only one person could go to Rome, Italy and I told myself I wanted to go there, for the history of Rome. My colleagues told me, **come on man, it's not gonna be easy**. I said **it's not impossible either**. I asked for more information about it and I had two months to get ready to prepare for the interview.

It was one of the biggest interviews I've ever done in my life, with more than ten professors on the circle table and just me in the middle. ☺ I felt so small. They started to ask me a lot of questions about myself, about my studies, about my dreams and why I wanted to have this experience. I was so nervous and excited that all I remember for that interview was, "We wish to have more students like you, to send them to Europe. Thank you for your participation." I walked out of the meeting room without an answer, with just hope in my heart that they would say yes to me. You may not believe it, but after two days I received the results.

The person nominated to go to Rome to study for six months was me! I started to cry and I realised how powerful thoughts of believing can be; that what you wish for can happen. And from that moment I became such a positive person. I started to hope more for everything in my life. I understood from that experience that preparation and the right mindset are everything.

So, my friend, dream BIG, wish, hope and work it out; you are in charge. Work hard on yourself to make a difference in your life, to live your dreams and to have what you want in life. I shared a few of my personal experiences just to help you and inspire you more about dreaming big, big, big, to scare you out of your complacency. I love this because it's so powerful and it makes you feel unique in this world.

Now you have an idea about dreaming, but this is just the beginning. No matter how old you are, listen to me, don't give up on your dreams. Your mind is just trying to find any excuse to not make it happen, okay? Remember, the mind is basing your capability and the potential outcome of your dreams on your past experiences. You must realign your thoughts so that the mind believes you have already succeeded at the task. The mind can't tell the difference between what actually happened and what you tell it has happened. With enough repetition, it will believe either way.

You have the right to dream until you die and after, if that's possible. Now starts the interesting part of dreaming. Remember, dreaming is not enough. It is for this reason that I have designed a special chapter where you will learn how to convert your dreams into goals and your goals into results. See chapter 16

You will find a lot of different people along the way who will try to drag you down, to influence you, to stop you; don't allow these people to make your life harder. Be selective, be assertive with the people in your life. It's really important that you assess the kind of people you spend most of your time with, who you speak to about your dreams, plans and desires. Select the most positive and enthusiastic people, those who love life and understand the meaning of it, the ones who can help guide you, inspire you, motivate you, critique you, and of course support you, the ones who will tell you the truth even if you don't like it, the real people who can see you as part of their family. It may be hard to find these people, but push yourself to do it, to make your life easier so you can enjoy it.

I remember myself ten years ago, having a lot of negative people in my network of friends. These people were without perspective about their future and their life, and I was in a difficult situation. I used to think like them, to blame, to make excuses every day. I used to say that life is hard and I can't do anything about it; I couldn't see any beauty I life, but year by year, I started to travel, to meet new people and to discover new cultures. I made new friends with different energies and mindsets and I started to follow their example and to emulate them. I started to love life, to see it as a miracle and every day as an opportunity to do my best, to help, to support, to inspire, to lead by my example. Now I've fallen in love with life and that's the reason I wanted to write this book for you. I wanted to give you another perspective on life. At the end of the day, my friend, the choice about how you want to live is yours.

I don't know where you are in your life right now, whether you are over 50 or under 20, rich or poor, happy or frustrated, but I know that this book will give you inspiration and will help you to change if you choose to. You have that power, but you must make the choice.

Dare to dream and do it properly. Dream big, my friend. Maybe you haven't before, but here is the beauty the Universal Law of Attraction – whatever you have or are today is the result of your dreams or other people's dreams. It's the result of what you've allowed to happen or what you've caused to happen by your thoughts. Think about it, if you are not happy with your life and who you are, it means that there is a big problem; you allowed someone else chose for you – who to become and what to have – they chose for you to work for their dreams.

You want to make your dreams work for **you**. So to become a big dreamer, you need to behave like a big dreamer and create the context around you to allow you to dream, to believe that it can happen, to think positively and to surround yourself with likeminded people who will encourage you to dream.

In the next chapter, I will share with you all the tools and strategies for how to convert your dreams into goals and goals into results, because at the end of the day this is all you need, all that matters. Remember, progress equals happiness, so if you want to be happy, you must have results that make you happy.

In the next chapter, you will learn how to become an achiever, how to educate yourself to step up from dreamer to achiever. This is so powerful and I'm sure will change your life forever.

Get yourself ready for the last session and the last chapter of this book. If you start to apply everything you find in this book, you will enjoy your life and you will become the person that you always dreamed of being. All you need is time and a lot of determination and ambition to focus on what you need to do to become a better person. Don't waste your time, it will never come back. Do what you can do today and try to live in the present moment as much as you can. Hope for better and try to see something good in every experience along the way.

Let's speak soon.

Do your best.

Chapter 16.

TRANSFORMING YOUR DREAMS INTO GOALS AND REALITIES

"The future belongs to those who believe in the beauty of their dreams."
Eleanor Roosevelt

I want to welcome you to this last session of this book where you are going to learn about how to transform your dreams into goals and your goals into results. One of the reasons why a lot of people give up on their dreams and stop seeking for better in their life is because they don't know what to do about their dreams; they can't see any goal or don't know how to set one.

Are you one of those people?

Are you one of those people who always has very good ideas, but never ends with anything concrete? Or are you a person that really steps up and starts to convert your dreams into goals? Which kind of person are you? Be honest with yourself. Are you just a dreamer? Or just an achiever of someone else's goals?

Or are you productive person that has both a dream and the willingness to manifest that dream by setting up goals and concrete plans to achieve that?

After years and years of following successful people, reading their books and following their seminars, I understood why most people are not achieving anything great in their life apart from the minimum that the social system has for them: school, degree, family, kids, maybe a house, then retirement. For most of us, unfortunately, life finishes there. I understood why most of us give up on our dreams and goals; there is something really important missing and that's one of the reasons I chose to write this book for you.

We don't receive any education about dreams and goals, except possibly at the college level, but many people don't go to college, and even if they are fortunate enough to do so, they may not take the courses that talk about setting goals.

We talked in the previous chapter about what dreams are and how we can learn to dream. I hope you've already started to dream again, the way you did when you were a child and dreamed a lot.

In this final chapter I want to focus on goals: **how to set up your goals and how to reach them**. This is the part people miss. I will share with you step by step how to take a dream and design it into a goal, to make a plan and get results from it.

I remember being frustrated for many years looking for results. I didn't know why I wasn't getting the results I needed until one day I started to do some research. I wanted to find out the difference between the poorest people and the most successful people, between happy people and unhappy people, the difference between dreamers and achievers. What I found out scared me and I started immediately taking the actions I needed to be a successful person. I started to implement all the strategies and tools that most successful people were using to get great results in both their personal and professional lives. I started to have local mentors and later global mentors and I started to look for opportunities to work on my personal skills. I invested a lot of time, energy and money into becoming an achiever so I would understand how to transform my dreams into goals.

So what is a goal and why is so important?

Very few people ask themselves this question, usually the ones who want to change their life, the ones who want to become leaders, the ones who want to add value to their life and help others to do the same.

A goal is a dream with a deadline.

A goal is something that you want to achieve, to accomplish, something that you want to shoot for **and you have made a plan for when you're going to have it**.

The difference between dreams and goals is a deadline. Let me give you a real example. If I want to lose weight and you keep repeating that to yourself, it's just a desire in your mind, nothing more. But if you say you want to lose 10 kg in three months, you have already given your brain more information for converting that dream/desire into a goal. Then you must create an action plan to achieve it, otherwise it remains an empty goal.

Later on, we will go through every single part of how to achieve your goals in life.

Goals are really important because they will create a sense of meaning in your life and keep you focused. You will then manage your energy toward that end through self-discipline.

Goals are important because they give direction for achieving your vision; we set goals because they are motivating and inspire us to keep moving forward toward a desirable end result; they become the force that drives us to achieve those great ideas we have in our lives.

Setting goals is one of the most powerful tools for helping us to grow, expand and learn. Goal-setting is the best strategy for helping you to accomplish just about anything.

If you want to become an achiever, you need to master the goal-setting tool.

To make this happen, you need to set an action plan. This is the part that's usually missing from most people's dreams, even if they do set a deadline/goal, and that's why they don't get the results they're looking for. Think about it; have you ever had in your life a real action plan? And if yes, did you follow it properly until the end of the course? This is the difference between successful people and unsuccessful people. I will share with you all you need to know to apply goal-setting so you can change your life.

Remember, you can know all the tools and strategies, but if you don't have a reason **why** you should do something, then there is no point to continuing. So train yourself to understand why you read this kind of book and what it is that you are looking for exactly.

Start with your vision. Make it simple and clear. If your desired end result is not clear in your mind and on paper, you will lose direction and focus and that will keep you from moving ahead. If you start to apply all that I'm sharing with you, all the success you are looking for is guaranteed; you can't miss if you commit to your goals, work hard, pay the price, go the extra mile and do whatever is required for you to accomplish your dreams and goals.

For more than 20 years, I lived without any goals or dreams; I used to do things just because I had to or because I saw other people doing them; I used to follow everyone that knew how to catch my attention and gave them all my energy, time, money and other resources just because I wasn't aware about my own potential, about my dreams and my goals. I didn't have any. I didn't really know who I was, where I was coming from or where I wanted to go. I had no idea about why I was here. None of these questions occurred to me until life pushed me over to the extreme side and forced me to change my mentality. I was forced to look deeper into life, into myself and to discover the meaning for me, for my own life. To me this was no coincidence. It was part of the magic of life.

I remember how difficult it was in the beginning. I had a lot of moments when I wanted to quit, I thought it was too hard for me, but it wasn't in the end. I got through it and that's why now I'm writing this powerful book: to inspire you to do the same; no matter where you are right now in your life, there is one single rule: **DON'T GIVE UP!** Your dreams, goals and plans are worth fighting for. It is worth discovering the real beauty, truth and meaning of life!

One of my mentors always said that people change or become aware and grow for two reasons: **either because they've suffered a lot and afterwards changed, or something happy changed them.** I think most of us change because of difficult situations, meaning we're generally forced into change, but happy occasions like the birth of a child or getting married can also cause changes in us.

Now, my friend, I'm honest with you, and because I care about your dreams and goals, even if maybe I don't know you in person (maybe one day I will see you in some of my seminars around the world), I want to tell you that you don't need to wait for some drama in your life to change you for better; you don't need to wait to become an orphan like I was, you don't need to grow up in the home protection like I was! You don't have to live on the streets or wait until you suffer some catastrophic event. You can change your life NOW from one of complacency to one of productivity and prosperity simply by looking at your dreams and giving them a plan for manifestation!!! You have to choose to do it: no one else will do it for you.

What are going to do now?

What are you thinking about?

What's your plan for tomorrow? Next week? Next month? Next year?

I want you to stop reading for a few minutes and do an exercise that really helped me understand what I wanted. You may not really love this kind of exercise, to write like a school kid, but this one is worthy and will be beneficial for you.

The exercise is simple.

You will forgot about your current situation and you will **write a letter about yourself to yourself**, with all the changes you want to make in your life, with all the dreams and goals you have, with all you feel you want to write down. Reread the letter now, when you're finished, then read it again next week, next month, next year or for Christmas or your birthday. Start now. It doesn't matter how much you write; what's most important is that you search the deepest inclinations of your heart and be honest with yourself. No one is there to judge you or make you feel small or stupid. Be honest and kind with yourself.

You can and should repeat this exercise many times throughout your life. Dreams and goals may change as others become real or your life shifts. In a few years, the goals you've set today may have all been fulfilled and you will want to set new goals based on your then current life. This is one of my favourite exercises!

Exercise: My Letter to me

Dear

_____

_____

_____

_____

_____

_____

_____

_____

_____

_____

_____

_____

_____

_____

_____

_____

Welcome back!

How do you feel now? Happy? Excited? Did you have fun? What did you discover? If you haven't done the exercise yet, there is no point in moving on. It's better to do it now. If you can't, put a note on this page and come back to it when you're ready.

I will share with you in the next pages the most powerful strategies and tools to accomplish your goals and dreams, all the same tools and strategies I teach my students in my seminars and courses. I will share them with you in this book. Be ready to take notes and to start to practice them today.

I have created a special guide for you to inspire and motivate you to take action, to move forward in your life, no matter what your situation is; if you follow my special guide properly, you will definitely achieve all your dreams, but for that to happen, remember, you need to commit yourself to doing the work. Most people try to avoid this part, and that's why they are still victims of their own prison and world view.

I put all I learnt about turning my life around into this book and I'm happy that you can read it and start to practice every single strategy. I'm sure not everything will suit you; it doesn't have to. Take just what you need to go for the next level. The objective is to level up, not inundate yourself or overwhelm yourself with demands that you can't or are not ready to fulfil. Take is slowly if need be. You have that power to make this happen.

Enjoy your guide.

Do better.

The power of goal setting and how to transform your goals into results in your life today

Everyone wants to be successful, but most people don't like to work all that much; this is typical of human nature. But in order to make a success of your life, to realise the potential you have and manifest your dreams into realities, you must focus on your self-development and do the hard work that will get you to the achievement of your goals. You need to do something to get yourself there before you can celebrate getting there. Before you see a positive outcome, you will be required to exercise self-discipline, gain education, do the homework, remain dedicated and put in the energy and time.

Each of these steps should be done in the order presented below.

The first thing to do is to create your vision board.

Create a vision board – Gather images and words that describe what you want to see in your future. Print from the computer or clip from magazines anything that can be put together into the package you call your dream. Be specific. If you want a house, what is the size, colour, how many rooms, where is it? Do you want a dog in the yard? A picket fence? A car in the drive? What kind? Paste all your words and images onto a board that can be put somewhere you will see it every day.

Once you have your board in place, view it several times a day. Remember, the human subconscious mind does not know the difference between what is real and what is not, so it will convert your images into what it sees as being real. When you can physically see your dream, it becomes more real and therefore more attainable.

I remember when I made my first vision board, more than four years ago. I put almost everything I could think of on it. It took a while to figure out what I wanted to do and how. I gave myself a bit more than my brain could handle at first. My advice to you is don't put more than ten dreams/goals per vision board. In this way, your mind will more easily sort and categorise these images. It's like the difference between reading an easy reader book and reading *War and Peace*. You may not be able to handle it all on a daily basis. But that is completely subjective.

Do what you think you can handle. You need to see it every day. Put it somewhere that you pass by all the time so you will get inspiration and motivation.

Now that you have your vision board with all your different dreams and colours, you have to pass to the next step. It is one of the most important. You need to write it down.

Write it down – this is the step that reinforces what you've put into your subconscious through your vision board. Each step is equally important to the others.

Once you have the vision board ready, look at it and prioritise your goals and dreams, then write them down. You have to write them down because, once again, this reinforces what the mind has seen. If you remember your early schooling, you may have been told that the best way to remember what you were being taught was to **read it, say it, write it**. When you do that, it creates extreme clarity and gives powerful energy to those images. It helps to connect your mind with your heart, where emotion gives even more energy to the visions on the board.

This is how you can unlock your inner potential: **See it, say it, and write it down.**

Write with as much detail as possible and read it every single day. This causes the subconscious mind to believe that the information it's receiving every day is real. Read out loud. This is 'saying it'.

Now you are ready to pass into the next strategy.

Break it down – No matter how big or small your goal is, you need to keep track of its progression. One of the reasons people don't accomplish anything in their life is because they see their dreams as being too big – bigger than they are.

If you break your goals down into manageable pieces or tasks, you will not become overwhelmed. Do these tasks daily so that you chip away at the big picture, working constantly to get to the end of that goal. Failure is not an option for you. If you hit a snag (something in your plan is wrong or doesn't work), keep moving forward until you succeed. Allow your plan some flexibility. Rearrange tasks, find new resources and do whatever you need to do to get it to work!

If you don't break it down, you may become overwhelmed and give up because it will all seem too much for you. This is one of the golden rules if you want to achieve your goals.

You need now the last and most important part of goal setting: **your action plan.**

Create an action plan – this is the element that's missing from most goal-setting. The dream or goal itself without any action plan will not help you accomplish anything. You have to actually do something to make it happen.

Though **goal-setting**, the **break down** and the **action plan** may seem similar because they all involve making something happen, they differ.

- **Goal-setting** shows you **what needs to be achieved**.
- The **break down** shows you **the order in which things need to be done**.
- The **action plan sets a timeline** for each portion of the break down and an overall timeline for completing all the tasks involved in your plan.

Create the action plan that suits you and your current available time. Most of us can't quit our jobs or abandon our kids to work on our dreams, so do your best. Give up some of your social life or other hobbies so you will have more time to work on your real goals.

Look at how you've broken down your goal into separate tasks, then create daily, weekly and monthly timelines for getting those tasks done. It may be difficult to see a year into the future for this, so if you're setting a long term goal that you feel will take you more than a year to achieve, keep the end result in mind; take it one step at a time. Do your research. Know what needs to be done first so you'll know what to do second and so on. And don't forget to be flexible. Particularly when setting long term goals, there may be tasks that you will find just don't work and you might need to adjust as you go along.

Be honest with yourself about the effort that you want to put in during the action plan. You won't go far if you don't have a plan that's **clear, practical, flexible and enjoyable**.

Make sure you understand your needs and what will work for you and that you are not just copying someone else.

I will share now with you a methodology that I usually use at my seminars about how to set goals using the S.M.A.R.T. system. It's a methodology that many coaches around the world have been using for more than 20 years and it's really practical and easy to use. (The first-known use of the term occurs in the November 1981 issue of Management Review by George T. Doran.)

Let's have a look and to start to set up your S.M.A.R.T. goals.
Good luck.
Do your best.

How to create S.M.A.R.T goals

Now you know all the steps to creating a goal from your dream and working toward a desired result. Many people set goals, but not smart ones. Since I started using this S.M.A.R.T. methodology, I've consistently seen results both personally and with my clients.

I will choose a real goal as an example to demonstrate how to use the S.M.A.R.T. methodology to achieve all your goals, no matter which area you've chosen to shoot for.

This year I will run a marathon for the first time. I'm actually going to run the Virgin London Marathon for the Hope Foundation, an organization that supports street children in Kalkota, Calcutta, India. I needed to set up a proper six month training **plan of action** so I would be fit enough to successfully reach the goal – completing this marathon. I've used the S.M.A.R.T. methodology for other goals and had great results, so I decided to use it for this one as well.

Let me explain **S.M.A.R.T** using my own goal of successfully completing the Virgin London Marathon.

What is **S.M.A.R.T**?

(S) – Specific

Everything starts from here. You want your goal to be very specific, so here you add more details about your goal:

- I will run the Virgin London Marathon
- It is a flat terrain marathon on the roads of London
- More than 45,000 people will run in this marathon
- The marathon will start at 10:00 in the morning
- BBC television and all the major world media will be there live allowing fans everywhere to support us.
- Hopefully it will be a sunny day.
- I intend to run this London Marathon for the Hope Foundation, for my family, for you, to inspire you to live a healthy life, and for the world, to bring hope, and to connect with more people.
- I'm going to smash this marathon; I want to finish in under four hours, and for me this is a big challenge, definitely going out of my comfort zone.

This is how you need to look at your goals, using as many details as you can think of, as many details as possible.

(M) – Measurable

You can't monitor something if you can't measure its progress; you can't change it or improve it if you don't know where it started and how it ended. Your goal needs to be measurable and to do that, you need data and information about your goal:

- I will train for the marathon six days per week.
- I will go to the gym two days a week and have two days of running intervals.
- I will run one 10 km run and one long 20 km run per week.

You must be able to hold your activities up to a measure. In other words, exactly when and for how long do you need for each portion or task in your plan? Do you need one day to collect materials? One week to draw a schematic? Two days to visit resources? Whatever it is, you must set a timeline or time frame for each of the steps, something by which you can measure your progress.

(A) – Active

There are two kinds of goal, **passive goals** (I will buy a house **when** my wife wins the lottery) and **active goals** (**this year** I'm going to run the London Marathon).

For the first type, you don't have any power or control; you are not in charge of the outcome. You are simply waiting for something random to happen before you take the next step to reaching your goal. You are passive, not actively working toward a goal.

In the second type, you have given yourself 100% of the responsibility for making it happen. You have the power to act toward your goal and you are using it by setting a timeframe for that goal.

To become an achiever, you need to set up all your goals as active goals. Now ask yourself if your goals are passive or active. Make the changes you need now.

(R) – Realistic

This is one of the most important steps and it's one that's often missing. You will become very frustrated if you've set unrealistic goals. You need to be honest with yourself. If you set a goal of earning a million pounds over the next month selling newspapers, that's probably very unrealistic (unless, perhaps, you actually own a major newspaper). Know your limits but don't set those limits too close. Allow yourself some expansion room. Don't overestimate or underestimate yourself, be honest.

I asked myself: **Do I think I can run the marathon this year? Yes, of course, if I train well and I follow the plan I can do it!** But if I were 98 years old with some health problems, maybe a heart condition and severe arthritis in my knees, would I realistically be able to do it? Or am I going to die trying?

Be realistic!

(T) – Time Bound

This is one of the most important steps of this methodology. Call it a timetable if you prefer, but you need to know when your goal is starting and when it will finish.

Starting is always the easiest part of any new routine, but most people don't set a finishing line – an actual time frame in which their plan needs to be fulfilled.

For example, you may know that you want to start going to the gym tomorrow because you want to lose weight, but you don't know when you will stop going because you don't know how much weight you want to lose.

I started my training for the marathon on the 25th of October, 2016, and I will finish on the 23rd of April, 2017. I'm training five or six times per week and I make sure I can see my performance going up. My deadline is the most important part of my goal. I need to know when my deadline is so I can focus on sticking to my timeline.

When you set up a goal, first look at when you need to be at deadline and take it from there. Like one of my mentors always said, "Start with the end in mind". I love this! I remember it every time I have to set up a goal in my life, no matter if it's big or small.

- Write down your goals and start to make a plan for how you're going to achieve them.
- Translate your vision board into words with as much detail as you can muster.
- Break down what you've written into an end goal, with tasks along the way to get to that end.
- Then give a timeline to your breakdown. Decide realistically when you want to complete this goal and give each task a period of time to be completed.

In this way, you will avoid procrastinating and stay focused on what you need to do.

You now have all the tools and strategies you need to successful reach any goal.

YOU CAN DO IT!

MY TOP 50 FAVOURITE INSPIRATIONAL QUOTES

"You can create your own quote to inspire you."
— Ionutcoach

I love to read books and remember the best quotes from them. You know how it is. Sometimes you can't remember everything, but you remember the highlights of the book. After a few years reading books, I started to fall in love with quotes and every single day I had a different one to inspire me. Over the last few years, I have collected thousands of quotes and I can tell you, my friend, that it has really been work. I try to learn from and practice every single quote. If you read my collection below and do the same, after a while I'm sure you will be able to create your own list.

Now, enjoy my top 50 inspirational quotes. I will start with one of my own. ☺

1. *"If you want to achieve your dreams and goals stop asking for permission."*
   — Ionutcoach

2. *"All our dreams can come true if we have the courage to pursue them."*
   — Walt Disney

3. *"If you do what you always did, you will get what you always got."*
   — Anonymous

4. *"Opportunities don't happen, you create them".*
— Chris Grosser

5. *"The ones who are crazy enough to think they can change the world are the ones who do."*
— Anonymous

6. *"The meaning of life is to find your gift. The purpose of life is to give it away."*
— Anonymous

7. *"Your problem isn't the problem. Your reaction is the problem."*
— Anonymous

8. *"All progress takes place outside the comfort zone."*
— Michael John Bobak

9. *"Too many of us are not living our dreams because we are living our fears."*
— Les Brown

10. *"If you don't design your own life plan, chances are you'll fall into someone else's plan. And guess what they have planned for you? Not much."*
— Jim Rohn

11. *"Motivation is what gets you started. Habit is what keeps you going."*
— Jim Ryun.

12. *"Enjoy the little things in life, for one day you may look back and realise they were the big things."*
— Robert Breault

13. *"All life is an experiment. The more experiments you make the better."*
— Ralph Waldo Emerson

14. *"Life is a game, play it; Life is a challenge, meet it; Life is an opportunity, capture it."*
— Unknown

15. *"The journey of a thousand miles begins with one step."*
    – Lao Tzu

16. *"The only way to do great work is to love what you do."*
    – Steve Jobs

17. *"To live a creative life, we must lose our fear of being wrong."*
    – Anonymous

18. *"If you are not willing to risk the usual you will have to settle for the ordinary."*
    – Jim Rohn

19. *"Take up one idea. Make that one idea your life – think of it, dream of it, live on that idea. Let the brain, muscles, nerves, every part of your body, be full of that idea, and just leave every other idea alone. This is the way to success."*
    – Swami Vivekananda

20. *"Opportunities don't happen, you create them."*
    – Chris Grosser

21. *"I have not failed. I've just found 10,000 ways that won't work."*
    – Thomas A. Edison

22. *"No one can make you feel inferior without your consent."*
    – Eleanor Roosevelt

23. *"Don't be afraid to give up the good to go for the great."*
    – John D. Rockefeller

24. *"If you can't explain it simply, you don't understand it well enough."*
    – Albert Einstein

25. *"Do one thing every day that scares you."*
    – Anonymous

26. *"The dreamers are the saviours of the world."*
    – James Allen

27. *"It is never too late to be what you might have been."*
– George Eliot

28. *"Believe in yourself! Have faith in your abilities! Without a humble but reasonable confidence in your own powers you cannot be successful or happy."*
– Norman Vincent Peale

29. *"Knowing is not enough; we must apply. Willing is not enough; we must do."*
– Johann Wolfgang von Goethe

30. *"The secret of getting ahead is getting started."*
– Mark Twain

31. *"Start where you are. Use what you have. Do what you can."*
– Arthur Ashe

32. *"Quality is not an act, it is a habit."*
– Aristotle

33. *"Be kind whenever possible. It is always possible."*
– Dalai Lama

34. *"When something is important enough, you do it even if the odds are not in your favour."*
– Elon Musk

35. *"Motivation is the art of getting people to do what you want them to do because they want to do it."*
– Dwight D. Eisenhower

36. *"I am not afraid... I was born to do this."*
– Joan of Arc

37. *"Deserve your dream."*
– Octavio Paz

38. *"You have to make it happen."*
– Denis Diderot

39. *"The way to get started is to quit talking and begin doing."*
    – Walt Disney

40. *"The past cannot be changed. The future is yet in your power".*
    – Unknown

41. *"Only the educated are free."*
    – Epictetus

42. *"I attribute my success to this – I never gave or took any excuse."*
    – Florence Nightingale

43. *"True happiness involves the full use of one's power and talents."*
    – John W. Gardner

44. *"Either I will find a way, or I will make one."*
    – Philip Sidney

45. *"Well done is better than well said."*
    – B. Tracy

46. *"You may delay time but time will not."*
    – Benjamin Franklin

47. *"Always desire to learn something useful."*
    – Sophocles

48. *"Success is no accident. It is hard work, perseverance, learning, studying, sacrifice and most of all, love of what you are doing or learning to do."*
    – Pele

49. *"A strong, positive self-image is the best possible preparation for success."*
    – Joyce Brothers

50. *"Success is where preparation and opportunity meet."*
    – Bobby Unser

MY TOP 6 CORE HABITS FOR SUCCESS

"We are what we repeatedly do. Excellence, than, is not an act but a habit."
– Aristotle

I remember myself before I started my journey into personal growth and self-education and I can see now that I was a different person. I used to react to situations, not act with reason behind my actions. I was a lazy person and I procrastinated most of the time. I often did not keep my word and I usually did what other people told me was good for me. I was like sheep following others without knowing where they were going or why. I didn't know anything about myself and my potential, about how brilliant I can be, how organised and productive a person can be, or what it meant to be a best friend and good person. I discovered another me actually and this was a big revelation. I'm being honest with you, my friend. The same thing may happen to you if you are not already aware about **YOU**!

One of the best things I learnt from my personal growth journey is to recognise, change and improve my habits. Once you are able change your habits and/or create new ones, your life will change 100%. I want to share with you my Top 6 most successful habits. I have many more, but I want to share the ones that I repeat almost every day.

When I started to study the power of habits and understand that almost everything we do is 90% out of habit, I opened my eyes and my mind. I started to ask questions about it and found new ways to change my habits; it's not easy to do. Some of you may need help from a mentor; some habits you can change on your own, some of them can just be improved and the best ones are the ones that you realise you want and need to grow and move forward in your life.

One of the reasons why most people are stuck and not getting the results they're looking for is because they repeat the same things every day and they expect different results. But to have different results you need to do things differently.

Some of the habits that you want to change may take you a minute, some a few days and some a few months, it depends on the habit, how strong it is and the meaning that it has for you. It's generally accepted, however, that developing a new habit takes about 21 days of repetition before it will take hold.

Let's do a quick exercise that involves just a bit of visualisation about your actual situation, about your daily habits, whatever you are not happy with, what you really want to achieve and who or where you want to be.

Think about your actual habits.
- Will they help you to get where you want to be?
- Do you need to change them?
- Do you need to create new ones?

It's such a simple exercise, but at the same time it's very powerful. Every time I start a new journey, make a new plan or set a new goal, I check if my habits are going to help me get there or if I need to create new ones.

Now you know why people don't have what they want and continue to complain about it. It's what they don't know that will keep them from achieving their goals and dreams. Good habits will help you become what you want, so be really careful with them.

Here is another exercise for you to do; this one will help you to identify your habits and understand why they are so important. Stop reading now and do this exercise.

Write two lists of your habits. Write down whatever number matches your number of habits.

- In the first list, write five bad habits that you want to change.
- In the second list, write another five that you want to create. They can be new habits entirely or they can improve upon a bad habit in list one.

This will allow you to see and change your habits and you can measure your progress. Habits are difficult to break, so start with one habit at the time. The more you master your habits, the more you will shine and be brilliant.

Here are your two lists of habits.

BAD HABITS   **GOOD HABITS**

1. _____   1. _____

2. _____   2. _____

3. _____   3. _____

4. _____   4. _____

5. _____   5. _____

I assume you've done the exercise. ☺ How do you feel? Please be honest with yourself. Honesty about self-examination is key if you want to grow.

I started to work on my habits at age 22. Now I'm 28 and I'm still working really hard with some of my habits. This is a long process and should continue throughout your lifetime. I can say that I have mastered some of them and some I'm still struggling with. Some are new and some are old, but together they've helped me to be the person that I am today, and I'm so grateful for my good habits.

I will share with you now my most powerful habits. I don't usually share these, but feel free to try them, copy or adapt them, or make new ones. Whatever you like.

1. KEEP A DAILY JOURNAL

This is one of my favourite habits. The reason you're able to read this book – the reason it's available at all – is because of this daily habit that I started more than three years ago. I was not and am still not a professional writer. I don't know the technical side of writing a book, but I had a strong desire to write down everything that I had in my mind at that time.

I was having a down period in my life when I broke up with my then girlfriend, and I didn't have any close friends to speak about it with, so I started to write my feelings and what was happening in my life. I didn't have a job at that time, I had just finished my studies and I was in a new country. I was at the point where I wanted to begin my master's in Coaching, but I didn't have enough money, so I had to work two different jobs at the same time to pay for school. It was hard, but I did it! I had a strong WHY for what I wanted, so I knew that HOW to do it would soon present itself.

I started to write most of the time during my depression, when I found myself crying and felt alone. Day after day, for a few months, I wrote until I was raised up a bit and felt better. By that time, I started to like the feeling of writing my life on paper and from that moment until now I've haven't spent a day without writing what happened that day.

In the beginning, I used to write a few lines; after a while, it was half pages and then full pages and so on. Now I have full journals, like books, from every day of my life. I started to shape my writing and I created my own style which I'm so happy to share with you.

You don't need to be a professional writer to put down your thoughts and empty your mind; it will increase your mental performance, your self-esteem and your creativity. It's definitely one of the habits that you shouldn't leave out of your daily routine.

You don't need to write too many things in the beginning; keep it simple and write what really matters for you. Here's how I organise my daily writing routine.

- First, write how you feel today; be honest with yourself. This is really important because it will lead to showing you how you can change what you feel; focus on your emotions, feelings, where they come from and what would make you feel better.

- Second, clearly write down what you are going to do today. You have to know what you will do, like a daily 'to do' list; this allow you to focus on accomplishing your daily tasks.

- Third, write down who you will meet with today and why. It's important who you meet because everyone can teach you something.

- Fourth, write what you learnt in that day, your personal experiences. Write it down so you can follow your progress in order to improve, change and measure it.

- Fifth, write down what you are grateful for today. I'm sure there are thousands of reasons out there, but for you, and only what happened today is what matters for this exercise. What are you grateful for that happened today?

Steps 4 and 5 can be done in the evening, while steps 1 through 3 must be done before you start your day. If you don't want to write twice a day (I recommend that you do), write steps 4 and 5 the next morning. I started to write three reasons every day and after a while I started to write five and then ten reasons, but actually there is not limit. Feel free to do what you prefer.

Here's a real page of my personal journal as an example, but of course you will do it in your own style.

****

London

10:28

Home

TUESDAY 7 FEBRUARY 2017

Today's challenge: Be yourself

What a beautiful day!

I woke up a bit late today because last night I went for the first time to an event called "The Inspired Stage" with my friend Hayden. I met so many lovely people and beautiful souls. I saw Emel and Lucia, a few of my old friends, and I made some new ones.

I feel so good today, positive and full of energy. I want to do my best today. To shine. To be brilliant.

Today, I have a few important meetings on Skype, my training for the Virgin London Marathon and afterwards I will continue writing my book because I want to finish it by the end of April.

I connected this morning with my beautiful wife Mina and I want to connect with a few more beautiful people today even if they are not here.

I learnt that our thoughts are really important and if we are not aware of them, we don't know why we do what we do. I started to focus on what I'm thinking and whether those thoughts are useful and good for me.

Today, I am grateful for this magical day, for my family, for my friends, for my job, and for my lifestyle. Thank you Universe, Life, God, Energy for this amazing journey on Earth.

Live – Love – Dream

Ionutcoach

2. WAKE UP EARLY

Work hard, stay positive, and get up early. It's the best part of the day.
– G. Allen

I used to have a really big problem with waking up early when I was a child. I had to wake up at 6:30 am and get ready to go to school.

What about you? What's your own experience with waking up early? Do you like it? Love it? Is it easy for you? Or difficult? Are you an early person or a late person? You may wonder which one is better. My friend, here is the truth: it depends on your lifestyle, preference, culture, country, continent and any number of other factors that may influence this. It depends on your health condition as well, but in general most people wake up early because they have to; only some because they love too.

What about you? Which category do you fit into?

Under ideal conditions, you should wake up at dawn, when the first light of day comes streaming into your room, but we don't live under ideal conditions.

When I was young, I hated to wake up early. But when I started to attend University and I understood that I was on my own and I had to pay for my food, for my books, and all my other expenses, I realised that I had to do things that I didn't like. I had two part time jobs: one as a merchandiser in the supermarket and one as a marketer on the street encouraging people to taste products. That was 2009 in Bucharest, Romania.

I learnt from that experience that I really can learn new things. I realised I have a lot of potential to study, wake up early, go to my two jobs and volunteer with my favourite association, A.S.G., the geography students association. More than that, I used to have very good grades and passed my exams, finished some successful projects and received a lot of praise from my colleagues who asked me to tell them my secret. They wanted to know how I was able to achieve all of this, hold two jobs, and play football as well. I told them I work hard, I stay positive, I learn a lot from my experiences and I wake up early every single morning. I remember a close friend added: "Come on man, even Sunday morning?" And my answer was, "Yes, because I go to church." Some of them started to laugh and others had no reaction.

I used to wake up early morning at 5 am for almost two years and I remember one day waking up and feeling good, like today was going to be something special. I felt as though I was special. I realised that everything was possible because I had to wake up early, even if I didn't like it. As a reward, I started to enjoy waking up early. After a few months, I had trained my mind to wake up before my alarm rang. I had a great time during my studies and honestly, so far, it was one of the best times of my life; I learnt a lot and I fell in love with the habit of waking up early.

Later on, after University, I had ups and downs with waking up early, but when I started to read books and study psychology and understand about body systems and mind functions, I understood that I was doing the right thing. Most normal healthy people only need 7-8 hours of sleep each night and most successful people have this in common: THEY LOVE TO WAKE UP EARLY! When I learned this, I thought,

WOW! This is the SECRET! And I started to train my mind to wake up early again.

I remember two years ago, I was waking up at 4 am (not because I wanted to but because I had too, as I was working at Itsu, a Japanese sushi restaurant and every day I started at 6 am). This was, up to that point, one of the best exercises for me, to get back into that mindset of waking up early. When I changed jobs, I start to wake at 5 am every day and then I tried 6 am to see which one was better for me. At present, I flow between 5 and 6. It depends on the day and tasks, my goals and the month of the year.

Definitely waking up early changed my life forever and I highly recommend it to you, too. At least give it a try: **you never know if some magical things will happen in those early morning hours.** This is the habit that you should have in your top 10 list of good habits.

> *"The morning breeze has secrets to tell. Do not go back to sleep."*
> – Wayne Dyer

Now what about you my friend? What time do you wake up? Are you happy with it? Can you fit everything you need to do into your day? I love to say that every second is equal to one pound sterling. I ask you, **how much money do you want to invest or waste away every single day?** If you wake up one hour earlier than usual for 30 days, you will have had 30 hours extra to do what you love. Does this make sense to you? Now multiply 30 extra hours by 12 months (360 hours), and then 10 years (3,600 hours). Look at what your investment has given you in return! In 1 year you will have gained about 15 extra days. In 10 years, 150 extra days. Those are full, 24-hour days!

So, where are we now? This is the power of self-management that most of people call time management. I teach my students in my seminars about this, because now I can say that I'm in love with this habit of waking up early. It will help you in all aspects of your life and business. But I can only advise you. The choice is yours, my friend.

3. WORK OUT EVERYDAY

I have always been into sports. I remember being around seven and playing football with my close friends Alin, Florin, and Vasile in the front of my house. The best thing that I remember was putting my sister in the position of goalkeeper. She cried the entire time because she didn't want to be goalie. I used to call all my friends from my little street in the village to play every day after school. I remember going to play football without doing my homework first. I've been a rebel since I was little, always breaking the rules and living on my own terms.

Time flew by and after a couple of years, my parents left and we were literally taken and put in the home protection, even though we didn't accept it at all. But actually this one was one of the best choices that my parents had ever made for me, I realised later on. We had so many more opportunities in the home protection than we had at my parent's home, as we were a poor family, if not the poorest of our little village of Vizejdia.

At the orphanage in Lugoj, Romania, we had the opportunity to go to school and create a future for ourselves; to do something with our lives. I started to go to school in the morning, and in the evenings I took take acting and theatre classes for almost three years. Afterwards, I went to the local football club in Lugoj for more than four years. I arrived to play in the second division as a junior and I actually did very well, but in the end I chose to go to University to study, even though becoming a football player was at that time one of my dreams. I gave it up because I understood that I didn't have the kind of support I would need around me for that type of endeavour. That's why I chose to go to study.

You may wonder why I'm telling you all these things. It's because I've always trained to do some sport, to move and it became more serious while I was playing football at the Football Club. I trained twice each day, one at the gym in the morning and one at the stadium in the evening. I was in good shape mentally and physically.

To work out is a verb; it's the act of doing some physical activity that hones the body. No matter what you choose to do, jogging, running, fitness, body building, playing football or tennis or ping-pong, whatever you prefer, you are working out.

If you don't have money to go to the gym, do something at home. Even simple exercises will keep you fit and healthy. If you think you don't have time, make time; wake up 30 minutes early if you have to. Working out every day is one of the best habits you can have in your life.

When you work out, you move all your energy. Your body releases dopamine, the hormone that makes you feel good mentally. It effects the pleasure centre of the brain, causing the same reaction you get when you eat to satisfy some emotional need, smoke, drink, or have sex. If you use any of these for long periods of time to satisfy your emotional needs, the 'dopamine effect' can become kind of addicting. You don't have to work out like I do every day, but aim for at least three times per week, minimum 30 minutes per day. If you work out, you will help yourself to keep fit and healthy, mentally strong and motivated.

4. READ DAILY

If you are like me, you probably never liked to do your homework. You preferred to play games with friends or watch cartoons. My favourite one was *Tom & Gerry*. I didn't like books all that much back then and most of us didn't enjoy them because most of the teachers and educators didn't take the right approach; they didn't know how to explain the subjects in a way that would catch our attention.

I started to read books, apart from the ones required in high school, when I was in my 20s, in my second year at University. It was then that I began to realise the importance of reading. I had taken a Psychology course because I wanted to discover why my parents left, what happened and if it was my fault (because all the time I felt like a victim). I had actually started to buy books on the subject at the age of 16 and I started to read about communication, problems in the family, mental health and about human behaviour. All these books answered my questions about why all of this happened to me. Even if I had chosen to study geography and meteorology as my majors because I liked them so much, I fell in love with Psychology and I started to read a lot of books on the subject. Year after year, I created the habit of reading daily, even if it was for 10 minutes, 20 minutes, half an hour, or sometimes even an hour.

After I received my degree, I approached the personal growth industry. I already understood a lot about it and I was essentially there, but I started to self-educate more and help others. I didn't know there was something called a coach. I didn't know anything like this even existed.

Since I started to study how to become a coach, trainer and speaker, I started to read books every day and I've never stopped reading. It's one of my favourite, most powerful core habits.

You are what you read, what you eat, what you explore, what you think, what you do! Consciously choose to grow, to investigate and discover the beauty of this life by starting to read a book per month. You don't have to read a book per week as I am doing now, or a book per day like some are able to do. Don't compare yourself with others. You have your own personal journey that is beautiful and unique.

Start to read something in your field, or something that you are passionate about. It doesn't matter. Find something that interests you and start reading. Create a habit. Read consistently for at least 28 days in a row (or minimum 14 days). Choose a time that works for you and read at the same time every day. I prefer the morning because I'm more focused and can understand better what I'm reading.

When you read, a transformation takes place, a bio-chemical reaction that effects your entire body and mind. Reading is a worthy habit and it will help you open your mind and your heart, to know more about yourself and others, to find like-minded people, and to understand how this world works.

You need to develop that need to read in the same way you would develop any other habit. Ask yourself now:

- How many books have I read in my entire life?
- How many could I read?
- What can I learn and how can I become an expert?

I created my own library because I'm a curious person; I like to seek and gain knowledge in my field and other areas that I'm interested in, to expand my vision, and to learn new skills.

Read! Read! Read! This is my personal advice for you and you will discover that it's a habit that will make you a better person, more knowledgeable, more skilled, and definitely more positive towards obstacles and difficulties in your life; you will understand that everything is happening not to you, but for you.

5. MEDITATE/PRAY TWICE PER DAY

I want to make clear that I am not going to speak about religions or about your personal beliefs regardless of what you believe. I want to focus on the practice of quiet time alone with your thoughts, whatever that means spiritually for you. Okay?

My family was poor and had a lot of problems, but what our parents taught us was respect for people, animals and nature. They taught us how to be kind, and always tell the truth.

I remember being no more than six years old, and close to my house there was a house where people use to go and pray, read the Bible, and sing in the name of God. I remember going there every Sunday. I started to make it a habit with my sister and my mum even if my dad didn't want to come most of the time. There, I learnt how to pray and I learnt about me, others and about love. It was that kind of church. It had a very nice environment. I loved it; it's where I understood that there is something more than us; there is an energy, something bigger than all of us, no matter what you believe in or what name you have for God. You have to believe in something whether it is karma, God, universe, energy, or whatever you want. You need faith in your life if you want to overcome any of life's difficulties. Personally, I believe in God and I'm proud to say that because I've felt guided to Him my entire journey. I'm so grateful for all the miracles in my life.

After years, I started to read about the history of religions and I discovered that I don't want to be a religious person. I prefer rather to be a spiritual person and that's how I discovered meditation. I started to like it and now I have moments when I want to meditate and moments when I want to pray; usually I pray or meditate at least twice per day.

The reason I want you to create a habit of doing this is because the results and outcomes are fabulous; it's not just about you becoming an amazing spiritual person, it's about becoming more calm, happy and peaceful as well as help you craft a new vision about life, about yourself and about the world.

Maybe you are already meditating and praying or not, but train yourself to do it as a daily habit and you will see how powerful this habit can be.

You will inspire your family and friends to do the same when they notice the changes meditation can bring both physically and mentally.

When you pray or meditate, something magical happens within you. If you get into the habit of giving yourself enough time to get completely relaxed mentally, you will connect with your highest level of consciousness. It's all about the energy that flows through us. Allow yourself to have a new experience, to learn something new about yourself by exploring your inner consciousness. Decide whether you like it or not. No matter what you believe in, open your mind and your heart to learn more so you can become more. Here on earth we must continue to grow or die, there are no others ways. I'm speaking about spirit and not body, because physically we all will die.

Start today to experience the beauty of praying or meditating and you will see how your life will change for better. You will notice the changes in yourself and others may notice in you that positive change and positive energy.

6. KEEP STRONG CONNECTIONS WITH FAMILY AND FRIENDS

One of the biggest and most basic of human needs is to be loved and accepted, to be recognised and validated, to feel important and appreciated because we've made a difference in someone's life. For this session I want to speak with you about the strong connections with family and friends.

You spend the better part of life growing with your family, and after with your friends and so on, so the way you connect with them is really important. No matter what kind of rapport you have with your parents, sisters, brothers, significant others or loved ones, the connection cannot be disregarded but if the connection is causing you harm, then you have to let go.

Honestly ask yourself when was the last time you said 'I love you' to a member of your family without any reason, not as a reaction to something else, but just because you felt like that. Think about how many times in your life you didn't pay attention or you didn't care enough about your family and friends at times when you should have, when you knew they needed you or could have at least used your help, and you 'had other obligations' or 'were just relaxing and didn't want to be bothered'. Can you do better now?

Of course you can. Everyone has that ability, but many don't understand love from the point of higher consciousness or Godly love. Real, ethereal, higher consciousness is unemotional and beautiful; there are many adjectives to describe love! But all the ways we know about love and all the stories we've heard from friends or surmised in some other way to form our opinion of love is nothing if we haven't actually become love.

If you haven't experienced the euphoria that comes with the real stuff, you are not there yet. If you need help in this area, you can start here.

- Don't ask for love and stop pushing yourself to love when you don't feel it. This will cause you to slow down and notice yourself and how you interact with others. How do you love them? Can you find something worth loving in your circle of friends other than great company? The deeper understanding starts with respect, then go from there. You'll know love when you feel it.

- Choose to **become loving** and you will receive love. Once you become loving, you can give love because you will be love. You have made 'being loving' a habit, so it's become part of you. And by the way, this is not super-difficult to do. On a scale of 1-10, it's a 1 for the easiest transition process in habit forming. You may not be able to do this if you pick a difficult subject to begin with, like your old arch enemy, so it might be best to start with children. It's generally fairly easy to find something you love about each child you know well.

Why? Because children are closer to being loving, undisguised and unmarred by outside influences.

- Keep the connection with your friends and family strong. Family and friends would be the people who are closest to you, whether or not you're related. Carve out and make it a habit to spend time with them. Your goal should always be to build and keep a healthy rapport based on strong unconditional love.

- Give of yourself, your time, perhaps your resources without expecting anything in exchange. Care because you want to care. It's as simple as that. If you don't care, you don't have to care. But when you start within your own circle, you will eventually find it very easy to extend that caring to a wider circle of people. Don't look on it as a duty; look on it as a blessing.

I lost the connection with my family and friends many times and each time I felt heart broken. I lost enthusiasm for life even if I had a job, money and other things at the time. But for me, nothing material can buy the feeling of being there, connected with your family and friends. I learnt from my mistakes, however, and I found ways to reconnect and enjoy life with them.

Even though my parents left when I was a child, literally abandoning us and destroying the primary connection, I wanted to rebuild that connection. It took me more than six years to build it back again, but I succeeded because, well, I'm me. And I'm sure you can do it, too, if it's something you really want. No matter what happened there, love is worth rebuilding. It's the same with real friends. Real friends will always be there for you. Just show them real love and be there for them. It's simple to have a friend, but it's not easy to be a real friend.

No matter what happened or happens in your life, my advice to you is to keep the connection with your loved ones strong by making them part of your daily life. Spending time with each other will help you to grow as a family and improve the quality of all the relationships around you. You don't need to make such a big effort to do that either. Little things can build up a strong connection; you don't need to buy anything or sell anything. You just need you to be there, available to listen to them, to hug them, and to encourage them when they need it. All of us can do that. Start from today to show kindness, to show love, and to smile and hug people around you, and you will see that magical things will happen.

MY TOP 10 FAVOURITE BOOKS

"A room without books is like a body without a soul."
– Marcus Tullius Cicero

I first started reading books (other than textbooks) when I was 16 years old and in high school. My first book, after the ones for the classes, was the Bible. I remember a lot of my colleagues laughing about it and making jokes about me, but personally, what I discovered in the Bible, I couldn't find in any other books.

The Bible is still one of my favourite books even though I've read more than 500 books in my life. I've discovered it's the best investment I could ever have made in terms of my learning and growth. Now I'm in the habit of reading an average of one book per week, more or less.

I don't know if you love books or not, but you should start to read some books about something you are passionate about, something that will inspire you, motivate you, or that will teach you new skills so you can become a better person or improve your life in some way. You can find everything you want in books, billions of books, all waiting for you. Just choose a topic, chose a book and enjoy reading. Reading is the best way to invest your time, and at the same time be in the present moment like you are now, reading my book.

If you will create a habit by reading every single day of your life, you will improve your mental health, you will always learn something new; it makes you feel better and keeps you alive; reading is one of the most powerful habits that you can ever have in your life. Your mind needs "food", knowledge, like your body needs proper food. But, just like food, be careful what you put in. Don't allow others to put in what is not for you. Use your own power to be in charge of your own learning, doing what **you** want, when **you** want and how **you** want.

I have in my library a lot of books, but I will share with you 10 of the most powerful; the ones that really helped me change my life. I hope you will find them helpful and useful, too. Open your mind and your heart when you read, be focused; start with 10 minutes per day if that's all you can do, and increase your time by 10 minutes each week. I read about an hour per day, more or less a book per week, and as far as developing a habit, you can choose any amount of time according to your schedule. ☺

MY TOP TEN BOOKS

1. The Bible is definitely one of the most powerful books in the world. I was amazed by how many things about life and about myself I related to in this book, and how much insight I gained into human nature. I still often refer to it when need be because it's full of wisdom and knowledge.

It was my first book, but at the time it was also the only book I had. Though there are a lot of valuable stories and lessons to be gained from reading it outside of the theological context, it may not be for the beginner who is simply trying to develop the habit of reading. The language is archaic in the older texts, but even modern translations are long and in places written in metaphor.

2. Se Solo Potessi – 9 Domande Che Ti Cambierano La Vita – Max Formisano – This is the book that opened my heart, my mind and my way into a life of awareness, spirituality, life coaching and training; this is the first book that I read about self-development, personal growth and positivity. It is written by one of the most famous trainers and coaches in

Italy, the one and only (and my first mentor and friend), Max Formisano. If you have the opportunity to read this book, I assure you, it will change your life forever. It's a fabulous book. Read it!

3. Seven Habits of Highly Effective People – Stephen R. Covey – This is an incredible book that went a long way to helping make me the person I am today, and I still keep reading it; it's an in-depth study of the 7 timeless and universal principles – external natural laws – for building character and talks about not only aligning our values with what we want, but also with these universal principles. It teaches the skills you will need and provides tools for improving yourself so you can succeed in any area of your life. I highly recommend it as a unique book in the personal development industry.

4. The Power of Now – Eckhart Tolle – This is one of my top three books because it woke me up and taught me one of the most important lessons in this life – to live in the PRESENT MOMENT, HERE and NOW! It's a magical book, and if it's not in your personal library, make it the next book you add. You will love to read this book again, again, and again.

5. Conversations with GOD – Neale Donald Walsch – I remember waking up in the middle of the night to read this book. Actually, this is more than a book. It's a series of conversations or dialogues Walsch has with God. You will love it; it's a fascinating look at our connection to all things and how easily the beautiful things in life can come to us when we know how to 'see'; one of the greatest books I've read. It can't miss in your collection.

6. Rich Dad, Poor Dad – Robert Kyosaki – I don't have enough words to describe this guide to developing your own financial freedom on this planet. This is the book that actually opened my eyes about the financial world, how it works and how to play in this big game, to fight for my financial freedom, the freedom that most of us just dream about! Buy it today and read it. You will learn how to change your mindset from one of poverty and lack to one of prosperity. Start to practice all the strategies to create a great financial life for yourself.

7. The Road Less Travelled – M. Scott Peck – This book is amazing if you are interested in the psychology of love and want to know more about spiritual growth. It will help you understand where you are on your journey and guide you to a new and higher level of self-understanding. I highly recommend you read this book; it's fantastic and you will love it.

8. Awaken the Giant Within – Tony Robbins – In this book Tony puts all the power and knowledge he has accumulated over 20 years of transforming people's lives, and he teaches you how to know yourself, how to find who you are, and where you're going. It will inspire you to ask for help and follow the examples, patterns, habits and routines of the most successful people if you want to be one of them. The book is full of techniques, tools and strategies that will help you in your personal and professional life.

9. Think and Grow Rich – Napoleon Hill – My personal opinion is that this amazing book is the best in the world after the Bible, depending on the arguments that you're interested in. It is a proper guide for you if you're looking for more in this life, if you want to grow and take your life to the next level. It's by far the best book for starting your journey into self-development. I still read this book when I think I need it or when I feel I'm losing my focus or direction; this book is a must in your library.

10. The Secret – Rhonda Byrne – This is by far one of the most magical books in this world, full of practices and advice for you to start to fly, to open your eyes and to understand the beauty and ease with which you can have anything you want in this life. It's all about intention and the Universal Law of Attraction. This book literally changed my life in less than a month and I'm sure it can do the same for you if you listen and follow the principles it contains. The book's underlying theme is the power of **believing** that something is possible in order to make it happen. If you don't believe, the universe if not going to work in that direction for you. *The Secret* teaches you how to believe in your own power, how to discover yourself and your potential. It will demonstrate for you the universal principles that guide us all. These are the miracles of life. I have to say that this book is one of the books that made me the person I am today. You have to read it at least once in your life.

P.S.

Live. Love. Dream. is meant to be your personal guide, to inspire and motivate you to find your way in life and if you are lucky enough and you've found it already, it will help you stay focused and on track, to flow and move forward. It's all about life skills and how to understand this game so you can be the best player.

I want to remind you that I wrote this book for three main reasons:

1. We are not too young or too old to follow our dreams, to live and love.
2. In schools and Universities they don't teach us how to live life, how to find a meaning to discover our passion and potential and to understand who we are and why we are here.
3. We all need inspiration and motivation. Anyone and everything can help us to change our life. It could be a movie, a person, a book etc.

I think no one is too young or too old to start to live their life, to discover love and to learn how to dream again.

The name of the book just came to me like a revelation, without thinking too much about a book title. Everything you find in this book is coming from my heart to your heart, to touch you so you start to believe in the power of life.

Throughout the book, I've been truthful with you about my life and my experiences; I wanted to inspire you to discover your potential and to make a difference in your life and the lives of others.

All my ideas in this book are really important for you regarding your personal development and your personal journey. My example has helped a lot of people to overcome obstacles and life difficulties, and I'm sure this book will help you, too. Sharing values with you, methods, techniques and tools to change your life for the better makes me feel like the happiest person in the world.

Remember, my friend, you have to be responsible and in charge of your life as well as your happiness, education health and wealth. You came here to shine, to learn, inspire, help, to love and to be brilliant.

Work harder on yourself than anything else; if you are lucky to find love, nurture it because it's rare; love with all your feelings, your body, and your mind. Keep your head up, no matter what, never give up on your dreams, your hopes, on your loved ones and, most importantly, never give up on yourself.

Take the best of every moment of your life.

Be the best you can be.

LIVE. LOVE. DREAM.

NOTES

_____

_____

_____

_____

_____

_____

_____

_____

_____

_____

_____

_____

_____

_____

_____

_____

_____

_____

ABOUT THE AUTHOR

Ionut Iulian Ungureanu born in 1989, Lugoj, and grew up in a small village in Vizejdia, Romania, until the age of 14, when his parents decided to leave him and his younger sister behind.

Today, he is an Inspirational Speaker, author of the book "Live. Love. Dream", the Real Results Coach and the Founder/CEO at Raise The World Company. His personal story and life journey inspires and motivates people to transform their life for better, to fight for their dreams, to achieve real results, and to live life with passion.

He is providing educational training, mentoring and personal coaching to both individuals and organisations since 2013. He designs seminars/ courses on a range of topics including Time Management, Public Speaking, Self-confidence, Achieving Goals.

His life motto is **"Never give up, you never know what you are capable until you jump out of your comfort zone and do it"**.

For more inspiration and motivation visit *www.ionutcoach.com*

EXTRA SPECIAL THANKS TO:

Isaia Nathanel

Catalina Chera

Antonio Malgieri

Ellen Kooimans

Patrick Constantis

Alexandra

Adina Oltean

Susan Watson

Angie Zapata

Zandela Soares

Ainara Leunda

Garry Grant

Marco

Shane Cousins

Natalia

David Hobson

Emma-Perry

Radha Dattani

Emil Iulian Iovan

Alexandra Badita

Davide Di Donato

Abdul Rahman Aloubaydi

Mastaneh Atighehchian

Ingrid Dover-Vidal

Claire Lockey

Dario Cucci

Liliana Nicolae

Sandra Islam

Leigh Thomas Brown

Kls Fuerte

Sidi Abale

Gianluigi de Bernardi

Margaret Donovon

Rosario Blue

P Ann Jackson

Carl P K Williams

Audrey Bossman

Ollie Trew